Care and Feeding of Volunteers

Barbara Bolton, Mike Bright & Byron Cressy

Care and Feeding of Volunteers

Recruiting, Training, and Keeping an Excellent Volunteer Ministry Staff

STANDARD PUBLISHING™

Cincinnati, Ohio

Standard Publishing, Cincinnati, Ohio
A division of Standex International Corporation
© 2001 by Standard Publishing

07 06 05 04 03 02 01   5 4 3 2

Information from the training session "Making Bible Memory Come Alive" was adapted from a workshop developed by Rod Brunson, Christian education consultant for Standard Publishing in Colorado. Used with permission.

Information from the training session "Why Johnny Can't Sit Still and Listen" was adapted from a workshop developed by Frank Mosley, Christian education consultant for Standard Publishing in Tennessee. Used with permission.

Dedication

+ + + + + + +

This book is dedicated to the memory of Dr. Cliff Schimmels,
a giant in the field of Christian education and a dear friend of Standard Publishing.

Table of Contents

+ + + + + + +

Chapter One

Caring for Volunteers Is Essential for Success

Jason has been involved in Christian education for more than thirty years. Recently he spoke at a major Christian education conference a number of times, training those who teach others. Almost weekly Jason speaks somewhere across the land, training and encouraging others to excel in the ministries to which God has called them.

Jason did not grow up in a Christian home, but at the age of five, he began going to Sunday school and church. Jason attended a little country church where Sunday school was held in curtained-off areas in different corners of the one-room structure.

Jason was from a large family, and there wasn't a lot of money for "extras." His family could not celebrate birthdays because there was no money for gifts. But Jason's sixth birthday fell on Sunday. His volunteer Sunday school teacher discovered that it was his birthday, and Sunday morning her Sunday school class included a birthday party for Jason, complete with cake and a blue-checkered shirt as a birthday present.

Jason's Sunday school teacher had a family of her own and did production work at a local factory during the week. She probably never realized the impact she made in that one individual's life. God himself only knows how many other lives were profoundly influenced by the ministry of one volunteer, factory-working homemaker.

Are volunteers important to the life of the church? Just ask Jason.

happen, but good leaders know how to make things happen. Have a plan!

If we truly believe that vision is from God and that our ministries are his, then we must commit to do whatever it takes to bring the vision to reality. No cost is too great and no commitment is too deep if we are doing his will. We must embrace our ministry vision with all the zeal and energy within us. We must embrace our vision with our people resources and with our budgets and facilities.

Vision, then, truly becomes the key to successful and productive ministries. If you don't have the vision of ministry, and you haven't caught the vision of ministry, then get out of the way of those who have. Someone once said, "Lead, follow, or get out of the way." That is good advice for the Church!

Build a Ministry of Excellence

✛ ✛ ✛ ✛ ✛ ✛

When you begin setting goals for your ministry, the most significant is to set a goal of excellence. In Kingdom work you must strive for excellence in all you do. The identifying mark of Christian ministry should be the mark of excellence.

God has always demanded the best of his people and has accepted no less. Even in Exodus 25, when the children of Israel were instructed to build the Tabernacle, a movable tent structure for worship, they were to use gold, silver, and only the finest of materials. God has always demanded the best of his people. Why then in our ministries do we recruit volunteers just to fill slots, fail to train them properly to develop ministry skills, and haphazardly choose the tools we give them with which to do the ministry? Much of what we do in ministry surely cannot be either pleasing or acceptable to God, whose very nature is excellent and perfect. Excellence must always be the benchmark of our ministries! It is important to keep in mind that our ministries are not about who we are, but who he is.

With excellence as the skeletal structure upon which we build all else, the next step is to set specific goals for our ministries. Remember that these goals come directly from our vision.

There are many kinds of goals and many areas where goals should be set. First of all, we need to determine long-range ministry goals. If you are the Christian education director or Sunday school superintendent, you must ask questions like "What is the overall purpose of our Christian education ministry, our Sunday school ministry, etc.?" Ephesians 4:11-16 can certainly give valuable insights into those questions. The scripture tells us that the gift of teaching is for the purpose of "making disciples" so that Jesus' followers might come to "maturity in Christ," discover their own gifts, and become a productive part of the body of Christ.

Once we determine the overall goal or purpose of our ministry, we need to set incremental goals. We need to determine where the ministry should be in ten years, in five years, in one year, in six months, etc. Establish realistic achievable goals and write them down. Realistic goals enable us to evaluate progress and measure success. Another old adage is "To fail to plan is to plan to fail." The reason old adages become old adages is that there is a great deal of truth in them. So, establish overall ministry goals, long-range goals, short-range goals, and even daily goals. But just as critical as goal setting is to record your goals—write them down! Constantly review the goals, and measure the ministry alongside its goals to keep it on target. Any ministry with no clear goals and objectives will soon become a frustration to everyone involved. (See the sample list of goals on pages 19, 20.)

As was mentioned earlier, out of our goals comes our ministry strategy. Strategy is simply the blueprint for achieving the goals, the plan of action. If the goal of the Sunday school ministry is to make disciples and to bring people to a maturity in Christ to the point where each Christian in the body is actively involved in ministry, then the question is, how do we make that happen? Part of that strategy certainly would be to set spiritual growth and behavioral goals for each department in the Sunday school. We would certainly need to choose a curriculum and provide other teaching tools and resources that would facilitate those goals. We would need to recruit teachers who understand the ministry of teaching and who will commit to that ministry. We would need to provide training that would enable those teachers to develop the skills they will need in the classroom. Strategy, then, clearly is developed out of the goal structure of the ministry, all the time keeping the goal of excellence foremost in the entire process.

Once our ministry strategy has been determined, we need to develop a process for evaluating the ministry. Many churches do a pretty good job of setting goals and even developing a strategy to achieve those goals, but they have no specific evaluation process. Evaluation gives us the ability to measure progress and to tweak or change strategy if what we are doing isn't working. If we fail to constantly evaluate our ministries, then we run the risk and probability of straying off track and losing sight of our goals.

Evaluation must take place in all areas of our ministry. We need to evaluate our strategy, our staff, our facilities, and our tools and resources. If we determine that we are not on target in achieving our goals, then we must determine where the weak link in the chain is. Did we fail to properly train our staff, or is the curriculum not what we need, etc.? Only when we constantly evaluate each area of ministry can we determine where and what our strengths and weaknesses are. We constantly need to identify and build on our strengths and strengthen our weaknesses.

The Teaching Ministry

✝ ✝ ✝ ✝ ✝ ✝ ✝

The scripture has a great deal to say about the teaching ministry. It is more than significant that when Jesus left heaven's throne and came to earth to live among men and to bring redemption and salvation, he came as a teacher. If you read the Gospels and study the teaching of Jesus, you will find that he used almost every teaching method, taught to the five senses, and understood learning styles. What a teacher!

In John 13:13-14, after Jesus had washed the disciples' feet, he claimed himself to be "Teacher" and "Lord." Throughout his ministry many called Jesus teacher and here in John, the very night before his death, Jesus not only called himself a teacher, but gave his disciples a compelling demonstration lesson of what it meant to be a servant. It is impossible to understand the emotion and physical stress Jesus was dealing with on this night, yet he never lost sight of the lesson. Staring a most horrible death in the face, he was still a teacher. He wasn't late to class, and he didn't stay home because he had too much to deal with. He was a teacher who understood his call and his ministry.

In Ephesians 4:11 Paul identifies the leadership gifts and lists teaching among them. Teaching is an essential part of the process for bringing Christians to maturity in Christ and enabling each follower to become a productive, functioning member of the body. The teaching ministry certainly carries with it a great deal of responsibility.

Much could be said about the teaching ministry, but perhaps James gives the best insight into this critical ministry. In James 3:1 he tells us "Not many of you should presume to be teachers, my brothers, because you know that we who teach will be judged more strictly." Wow! That should be a warning to us that God takes this Christian education ministry seriously. Teaching is the only ministry that the scripture attaches stricter judgment to. It is important to note that the teaching ministry incorporates the children's ministry, youth ministry, and the adult ministry. It is so very critical that we get it right. So much hinges on the teaching ministry.

The teaching ministry dramatically affects all aspects of church life. As we again examine Ephesians 4:11-16, we can easily see how the teaching ministry affects spiritual growth in individual Christians.

Teaching is a critical part of the process "to prepare God's people for works of service, so that the body of Christ may be built up until we all reach unity in the faith and in the knowledge of the Son of God and become mature, attaining to the whole measure of the fullness of Christ" (Ephesians 4:12, 13). If you have Christians in your church who are not involved in "works of service" or who are not mature in the faith, there is a real possibility that there is a problem or breakdown somewhere in your teaching ministry. Many churches in their children's Sunday school alone may use curriculum from four or five different publishers, each with a different scope and sequence. All of these may be good curricula, but we have butchered any plan for continuity in the spiritual development of our children by subjecting them to a hodge-podge of curricula with no clear, distinct scope and sequence. (See the sample curriculum evaluation checklist on pages 21, 22.)

Good teaching brings spiritual maturity in individuals so that they "will no longer be infants, tossed back and forth by the waves, and blown here and there by every wind of teaching and by the cunning and craftiness of men in their deceitful scheming" (Ephesians 4:14). Good teaching is foundational in the development of solid, mature believers. We must get it right!

The strength of church growth in any church is found in a good, solid teaching ministry. When we do a good job of teaching, and in turn develop spiritual maturity in individuals, then we build strong, solid congregations.

A strong, solid teaching ministry can have a significant impact on the evangelistic outreach of a congregation as well. One church in central Illinois realized just how much. The church is a fairly large congregation, and some time ago needed a teacher in a young couple's class. The class actually had about thirty couples in the class. Joe, the new teacher, took his new ministry seriously. He spent hours in preparation, even though he was a public school teacher with lots of preparation already to do, and a husband and father of four. Joe did a good job of building relationships with his class, and the church model of Ephesians 4:11-16 began to become a reality. The class began to love, encourage, and assist each other, and the community began to see a Sunday school class truly model a Christ-like spirit and behavior. The class began to grow. Over a period of time the class peaked at 247 people and averaged 178 per week. These new people were non-Christians who saw Jesus modeled in a Sunday school class. People want to go where they will be loved, welcomed, and accepted and where their needs are being met.

STRATEGY FOR GOAL SETTING

Step One—Vision

Step Two—The desire to reach the goal

Step Three—Prayer

Step Four—Belief that the goal can be achieved

Step Five—Determine the benefits of accomplishing the goal

Step Six—Analyze your present situation and status

Step Seven—Set a realistic deadline

Step Eight—Identify any obstacles you will have to overcome

Step Nine—Identify what knowledge you will require in order to accomplish the goal.

Step Ten—Identify all the people whose cooperation you will need to accomplish the goal

Step Eleven—Develop an action strategy from steps eight, nine, and ten

Step Twelve—Clearly visualize the end result

Step Thirteen—Saturate the process with determination and persistence

Step Fourteen—Give God the credit when the goal is reached

SAMPLE SHORT- AND LONG-RANGE GOALS

Every Day

Director prays for leaders/teachers in her ministry area.

Leaders/teachers pray for their groups/classes.

Teachers consider their lessons.

Director, leaders, and teachers are actively involved in personal spiritual exercises (prayer, reading the Bible, etc.).

Every Week

Director does a random check for problems among classes.

Make sure teachers are checking on absent students and/or checking into visitors.

Ministry leaders encourage the people in their groups to pray for each other throughout the week.

Director, leaders, and teachers should be watching for helps and tips in books and articles they are reading and share them with others.

Every Month

Director specifically checks for problems with each leader/teacher: students, space, curriculum, time, personal problems, etc.

Director distributes timely, helpful information he has gathered from his reading to all teachers, assistants, substitutes.

At least one ministry group reports recent accomplishments in the church newsletter or bulletin.

Every Quarter

Director holds some sort of "maintenance" training (brief sessions for discussing general business and for specific issues training).

Director gives general appraisal report to the church leader who is overseeing that specific ministry area (if the director is also a volunteer).

Director and church leader meet to discuss general concerns and to pray.

Plan for a way to recognize and encourage volunteers.

(continued)

SAMPLE SHORT- AND LONG-RANGE GOALS

Every Six Months

Prayer meeting for church leaders, director, teachers, assistants, substitutes, etc., to pray for the church, programs, students, and each other.

Church leader responsible for the ministry should be updated on progress or problems.

Specific training for special teaching situations: VBS, education programs, electives, etc.

Every Year

Hold a major in-house training event for all leaders, teachers, assistants, substitutes, and helpers with a person from outside the church; perhaps gather with volunteers from another church.

Give current volunteers opportunity to renew their commitment or to take a break or to quit.

Recruit volunteers to fill empty positions, at least one quarter before the next year begins.

Plan for next year's curriculum; evaluate possible replacements; select and order.

Hold a major volunteer appreciation event.

Evaluate teachers; complete at least in time to line up replacements if necessary.

Brainstorming session for expanding or improving education program.

Every Two Years

Evaluate entire ministry program.

Evaluate relationship of director with volunteers.

Evaluate recruiting procedures.

Evaluate volunteer training program.

Evaluate volunteer evaluation procedures.

CURRICULUM EVALUATION CHECKLIST

1. Lesson Objectives
❏ Lessons and units of lessons have clear, measurable objectives that plainly state what students will do as evidence of having learned the material.
❏ Lesson objectives support the vision, mission, and goals of the church's ministries.
❏ Lessons suggest activities that will clearly lead to the fulfillment of the stated lesson objectives.

2. Bible Content
❏ Lessons and related activities clearly present the Bible as God's authoritative, inspired Word.
❏ Lessons and related activities present Bible teachings and accounts accurately.
❏ Lessons do not impose interpretations on Bible teachings and accounts.
❏ Lessons give students opportunity and encouragement to investigate and study the Bible on their own.

3. Doctrinal Issues
❏ Lessons deal with doctrinal issues appropriately for our church.
❏ Lessons teach essential beliefs of our church.
❏ Lessons offer examples and illustrations of essential beliefs in ways that are appropriate or familiar to people in our church.

4. Life Application
❏ Lessons set apart specific time or activities in which the students actively consider how to apply the lesson truths to their own lives.
❏ Lessons encourage students to identify the practical aspects of each lesson and apply them to their own lives.
❏ Lessons suggest learning activities that empower students to apply the lesson truths to their own lives.

5. Teaching Methods
❏ Lessons provide a balance of teacher-based instruction and student-based learning.
❏ Lessons suggest a variety of learning activities that meet the needs of students who have different learning styles.
❏ Lessons utilize teaching methods that are widely used and are familiar to both teachers and students and allow for a blend of creative, innovative methods.

(continued)

For just a moment Mr. Johnson was caught off guard as David said, "Mr. Johnson, the mice will eat all the food and there won't be any left for the other animals." Mr. Johnson quickly regained his thoughts and assured David that he would keep an eye on the mice.

Mr. Johnson resumed the story of how the water got higher and higher and how the people began to panic as they realized the "crazy old man" wasn't crazy after all. Frantically, the people began to run to the mountain where the old man had a big boat.

It was at this point when four-year-old David again raised his hand and Mr. Johnson paused to call on him once more. David boldly pointed out to Mr. Johnson, "You're not watching the mice, and they will eat all the food, and there won't be any left for the other animals."

Determined to take David's mind off the two plastic mice, Mr. Johnson lifted the lid on the ark and placed the mice on the second floor out of sight. He said to David, "We'll put them upstairs away from the food supply." That seemed to please David for the time being, and Mr. Johnson enthusiastically resumed the Bible story with all the animation of an experienced storyteller.

Mr. Johnson was in the peak of excitement as he tried to relate the fear and panic of hundreds, perhaps thousands, of people who were running to the mountain where the old man and his boat could possibly save their miserable lives. And just then David raised his hand. As Mr. Johnson acknowledged David, the excited four-year-old exclaimed, "Mice can climb and they'll be right back down there in no time. Then they'll eat all the food and there won't be any for the other animals."

Mr. Johnson reluctantly removed the mice from the boat and placed them in his pocket, assuring David that they would not make this trip. And the story went on. Mr. Johnson had so taught the lesson that four-year-old David was living the adventure.

Helping People Find a Place of Service

✚ ✚ ✚ ✚ ✚ ✚

The nature of great teaching is the ability to bring students to a personal encounter with God's living Word. That's the kind of teacher we all want to recruit.

When Christian leaders are asked to identify their greatest ministry challenge, recruitment is usually their response! Let's define recruitment as the act of helping people in our churches find a meaningful place of service. It is not filling slots on a chart! Recruitment must become a continuous process. The goal of an effective recruitment strategy should be to have a list of volunteers ready to teach when the need arises. Many times, we wait until there is a need and then recruit in a panic. Panic recruitment destroys the joy of enabling people to become part of a meaningful ministry that utilizes their God-given gifts. Begin to establish a recruitment strategy for your ministry by trusting God to fulfill his promise in Matthew 9:37, 38, "Then he said to his disciples, 'The harvest is plentiful but the workers are few.' Ask the Lord of the harvest, therefore, to send out workers in his harvest field." The harvest is his. He will provide workers. Make prayer and trust integral parts of the recruitment process and God will provide!

Establish prayer teams. Develop prayer partners. Inform those who are praying of specific needs. Encourage them to call upon God to work in the lives of those workers he would have be a part of his teaching team.

Before a recruitment strategy can be put into place, effort must be made to create congregational awareness of the education program. Teacher, volunteer, and worker classes should not be words that are expressed only when there is a need for volunteers. Members of the congregation need to feel a part of an important program and ministry that is teaching God's Word to learners of all ages. We need to develop a sense of responsibility and ownership for everyone in the church family. Not everyone should be a classroom volunteer, but there are many support roles that need to be accomplished. Certainly, *everyone* can become part of the prayer team. Others may encourage. Some may assist in the preparation of materials. Still others may provide transportation. Regular, clear communication is necessary if these goals are to be accomplished.

Carefully plan the details of making congregational awareness a priority. Plan for a period of twelve months. Be sure the people responsible for sharing information know exactly what is to be communicated, when it is to be communicated, and how it is to be communicated. It is crucial to have quarterly communication. Actually, monthly communication will be far more effective.

You may wish to develop a note card with the following four statements on it. Ask volunteers, leaders, prayer partners, and others who are interested in communication to place the card in a place where they will see it several times a day. Ask God to provide insights and directions for ways to accomplish these four goals:

- share the vision,
- present the challenge,
- pray and work, and
- expect God to provide.

Specific Suggestions to Promote Congregational Awareness

+ + + + + + +

1. Frequent, short articles describing some activity of the education program should be included in every issue of newsletters that are sent to homes.

2. Bulletin board displays showing learners in action or projects completed by learners provide an effective method of communication.

3. Smiling teachers sharing something good that happened in class as they walk to their cars after a teaching session will help to share the joy of the education ministry.

4. Plan for volunteers to wear "Ask Me" buttons.

• Ask me about teaching third grade.

• Ask me about nursery laundry.

• Ask me about playground duty.

• Ask me about teaching Twos.

• Ask me about preparing teaching materials

5. Utilize bulletin inserts. Create your own monthly bookmarks that are reproducible. Fill in specific prayer requests. Insert in bulletins. Ask people to pray regularly and specifically for needs listed on the bookmarks. Suggest to the people that they should place the bookmarks in a Bible that they read on a regular basis.

Be aware of possible responses from people you contact

+ + + + + + +

What motivates people to volunteer? There are a number of different reasons. Some people volunteer because of a personal need (for personal fulfillment or because of an inherent personal belief, for example), and others may serve out of pragmatism (for example, they have a child in the program or they are already in the building at that time, so why not help?). The reasons are varied and sometimes quite complicated. Regardless of the reasons why people volunteer, you must be able to identify the reasons for what they are and be able to redirect each volunteer's energies or temper their motivations to better serve the people with whom they are ministering. This also helps you minister to your volunteers, giving them biblical reasons and motivations for serving and giving them opportunities to grow spiritually.

1. People want to serve God and the church family.

2. People want to support their belief system.

3. People want to be part of a significant program.

4. People want to be part of a team.

5. People want to demonstrate caring.

6. People want to be needed.

7. People want to make a difference.

8. People want to help others.

9. People want to develop new skills as well as use those they have.

Not only should you have an awareness of these needs, but be sure that prospects are aware of the potential for having all of these needs met when they become part of the teaching ministry. When you can address your needs for volunteers as benefits that meet their needs, you will find people who are more willing to serve, more capable of serving effectively, and more willing to make long-term commitments.

Six-Step Recruitment Strategy

✢ ✢ ✢ ✢ ✢ ✢ ✢

Step One: Gather Names

Prepare a list of names of people who are "suspects." They are not "prospects" at this point. They are simply individuals whom you have identified as someone who might consider a teaching ministry. It is not possible for one person to assemble an adequate or complete list of suspects. Enlist help.

Talk with staff members. Ask about people you don't know. Very often a staff member will know the greatest number of people in the congregation. A staff member may also be aware of reasons not to contact some people and, at the same time, name those who may be most likely to consider a teaching ministry. Staff communication also prevents any one individual from receiving a large number of contacts from a variety of ministries.

Ask teachers of adult classes for recommendations. We seem to think that teachers will not want class members to leave class to teach. On the contrary, they may be very willing to suggest names of those who are ready to become part of the teaching ministry. Also, consider that there are many opportunities for ministry that do not take learners from their adult classes.

Ask current teachers to suggest names of friends and acquaintances that need to be contacted and asked to consider the teaching ministry.

Invest some time in study of the church membership directory. Establish a goal to determine what contribution every member can make to the education ministry. There are many, many responsibilities that support the ministry. Next to each name in the directory, list hobbies, skills, and interests. Then determine how those people can contribute and serve others. For example, someone who sews can make smocks for the nursery workers and costumes for drama activities. Someone who enjoys video recording may be able to record sound effects and backgrounds that will enhance the telling of a Bible story. Think creatively!

Step 2: Make an initial contact

Inviting people to consider being part of the teaching ministry is so important that it must begin with an individual, face-to-face contact.

Call to make an appointment for a fifteen- minute conversation. Tell the person three or four times you can be available and ask them to select one of those times. You may meet at church or in the person's home. Make it as convenient as possible.

Begin the time with prayer. This will establish value and importance to your conversation. Explain that you are inviting the person to an informational meeting related to the teaching ministry. Be clear that you are not asking for a commitment for involvement, only a commitment to attend an informational meeting. If possible, have two dates for available meetings so that each person may select the most convenient time.

If your list of names is too long for one person to make the contacts, enlist a team. Two, three, or four people can make a large number of contacts in a relatively short period of time.

Step Three: Plan and conduct informational meetings

People who agree to attend an informational meeting are no longer suspects. They become prospects! Pray for each one individually. Ask God to help them recognize their giftedness and call and to be willing to follow his leading. Try some of the following tips to make your meetings more efficient and effective.

- Begin and end meetings on time.
- Prepare printed materials well in advance. Ask someone who is not familiar with the information to read for clarity.
- Arrange the meeting area so that those attending will feel comfortable and be encouraged to participate in questioning and discussion.

- Provide a biblical base for involvement in the teaching ministry. (Matthew 28:18-20; Romans 12:7; Ephesians 4:11-14; 2 Timothy 3:16).
- Share information about the following:
1. Specific ministry opportunities
2. Requirements
3. Job descriptions
4. Available support
5. Plan for equipping for success
6. Importance of relying on prayer when making decision
- Provide opportunity for questions and discussion.
- Determine a time when contact will be made for decision about involvement. Allow about seven to ten days before the next contact.
- Encourage prospects to call with questions and concerns during this time.

Step Four: Ask for commitment

Make follow-up contacts as planned. Expect that some will respond with enthusiasm and be ready to make a commitment to become part of a teaching ministry. Know that some will have additional questions. Answer right away or schedule another meeting, if that is necessary. Some prospects may offer reasons or stumbling blocks to their affirmative response.

- "I'm too busy." (Share support and resources that will help to lessen time needed. Resist the temptation to say, "It really won't take much time." Preparation DOES take time.)
- "I have too many other responsibilities." (Encourage the individual to evaluate use of time. Ask which responsibilities use that person's gifts most effectively. Consider ways to share some of the responsibilities.)
- "I've never taught before. I don't know how." (Discuss opportunities for equipping. Discuss teaching teams. Teach with an experienced teacher. Describe resources and available support.)
- "I'm retired and want to be free to travel." (Consider planning travel so that not too many weekends are involved. Explore a mid-week ministry. Ask about a support ministry with flexible scheduling.)
- "I taught for many years. Let someone else do it now." (Scripture does not teach that we serve for a time and then stop.) Colossians 3:16, 17 says, "Let the word of Christ dwell in you richly as you teach and admonish one another with all wisdom, and as you sing

psalms, hymns and spiritual songs with gratitude in your hearts to God. And whatever you do, whether in word or deed, do it all in the name of the Lord Jesus, giving thanks to God the Father through him."

If a prospect declines involvement in the teaching ministry, explore other ministry involvement. It may be helpful to ask the individual to complete a survey form. A sample "Church Family Survey" is provided on pages 32-34. Reproduce and use it as is or adapt it to meet the needs of your church family. When the surveys are completed, give names of people to be contacted to the appropriate ministry teams.

Individuals who volunteer to become part of the teaching ministry need to be asked to complete an information form. A suggested form is provided on pages 35, 36. It may be reproduced and used as is or be adapted to your specific ministry.

Step Five: Provide initial training

Volunteers will need information about the ages they will be teaching. They will need to be aware of behavior management techniques. Lesson planning skills will be important. Understanding of ways people learn, how to use curriculum, and a number of specific teaching methods will need to be developed.

- Assess specific needs of your volunteers.
- Plan for a variety of training experiences. More specific help will be provided in chapter three. Also, twelve teacher-enrichment sessions are provided in chapter 8.
- Some individual training will be needed.
- Teaching teams can be trained together.

Some topics can be helpful to all volunteers involved in the teaching ministry. The goal for training or teacher enrichment is to equip volunteers to be successful!

Step Six: Plan for observation

Observation of experienced teachers is a valuable training tool. Volunteers who have never been involved in teaching may wish to observe classes of a variety of age levels to help determine the age/grade groups most appropriate for their ministry.

Teaching alongside an experienced teacher in a team setting will provide effective on-the-job training. The new recruit may gradually assume responsibility for a portion of the teaching session until assuming full responsibility seems quite comfortable. More experienced teachers will be encouraged and stretched as they assume a mentoring role.

- Provide an observation form for new recruits to use. (See page 37.) Sometimes it is difficult to know what to look for and to know which observations are pertinent. Value of observation will be increased if there is opportunity to discuss the session with the teachers as well as the director or coordinator.
- Be available to volunteers for evaluation, encouragement, and expressions of successes as well as needs.

Continuous evaluation is essential to ensure growth of volunteers as well as meaningful learning experiences for students. Plan for regular times of evaluation as well as being available for conversation as the need arises.

Department Director or Coordinator

- Pray regularly and individually for volunteers in department.
- Be available to volunteers during sessions.
- Communicate with Christian education ministry team.
- Communicate with support directors.
- Observe strengths and weaknesses within each class.
- Assist with evaluation based on observations.
- Affirm and encourage volunteers.
- Communicate training needs to training director.
- Anticipate staff needs and communicate needs to recruitment director.

Recruitment Director

- Pray for recruitment of new workers.
- Develop a volunteer packet (part of a notebook to be kept) with the assistance of the Christian education ministry team.
- Communicate with department directors and teachers to determine recruitment needs.
- Work with the training director to schedule training for new workers.
- Evaluate effectiveness of recruitment strategy and adjust accordingly.

Training Director

- Communicate with directors and coordinators as needed.
- Communicate with promotion coordinator to promote teacher enrichment events.
- Communicate with department directors and teachers to determine training needs.
- Schedule teacher enrichment sessions as appropriate.
- Coordinate development and production of teacher handbook.
- Evaluate the effectiveness of training programs and adjust accordingly.
- Be aware of area training opportunities.

Support Ministries Director

- Build relationships with support ministries directors.
1. Communicate with each one as needed.
2. Provide prayer support.
3. Be available to respond to requests and needs.
- Evaluate effectiveness of each support ministry with the appropriate director.

Resource Director

- Keep resource room neat, clean, and organized.
- Receive supply and equipment requests from teachers.
- Provide teachers with an updated equipment inventory list as needed.
- Respond to supply and equipment requests in a timely manner.
- Purchase supplies and equipment as authorized.
- Maintain (or have maintained) all equipment in proper working order.
- Monitor equipment returns.

Promotions Director

- Communicate with department directors and teachers to determine promotions needs.
- Communicate with recruitment director as needed to support continuous recruitment strategy.
- Communicate with support ministries director as needed.
- Maintain an on-going promotions program for regular Sunday school attendance, as well as special events. Utilize a variety of media to promote events (bulletin, newsletter, Power Point, posters, flyers, etc).
- Evaluate the effectiveness of promotions programs and adjust accordingly.

TEACHER JOB DESCRIPTION

Lead Teacher (**LT**), Co-Teacher (**CT**), Teacher Helper (**TH**), and Substitute Teacher (**ST**)

	LT	CT	TH	ST
I. What the teacher is to be (Qualifications):				
A. Christian	√	√	√	√
B. Member of Church (minimum one year)	√	√	√	√
C. Regular in worship attendance	√	√	√	√
D. Yielded to the Lordship of Christ	√	√	√	√
II. What the teacher is to do (responsibilities) in relationship to:				
A. Students				
pray for	√	√	√	√
be on time to greet	√	√	√	√
know individually	√	√	√	√
develop profile of	√	√		
build relationship with students/families	√	√	√	√
plan outside activities with	√	√	√	opt.
encourage regular Sunday school attendance	√	√	√	
communicate with by mail and phone	√	√		
organize for ministry	√	√		
recognize visitors and make them feel welcome	√	√	√	
B. Classroom Teaching Team				
pray for each other	√	√	√	√
communicate with the team regularly and clearly	√	√	√	√
mentor	√			
coordinate lessons	√			
prepare quality, creative lessons	√	√		√
define roles and responsibilities	√			
be accountable to each other	√	√	√	√

(continued)

TEACHER JOB DESCRIPTION

	LT	CT	TH	ST
C. The Teacher's Department Director				
pray for	√	√	√	√
develop good relationship with	√	√	√	√
communicate needs	√	√	√	√
meet with	√	√	√	√
request resources from	√	√	√	√
ask questions of	√	√	√	√
communicate absences when additional staff is needed	√			
D. Curriculum				
order from department director	√			
become well acquainted with	√	√	√	√
have a basic understanding of the scope and sequence	√	√		
E. Meetings (1 to 1½ hours; regularly scheduled)				
be regular in attendance	√	√	√	√
be prepared	√	√	√	√
keep Christian education calendar handy	√	√	√	√
if unable to attend, contact department director for notes	√	√	√	√
F. Training				
participate in self study	√	√	√	√
participate in mini-training courses	√	√	√	√
communicate with training/resource people	√	√	√	√
G. Forms and Reports				
complete/maintain forms as appropriate				
student registration form			√	
attendance			√	
offering			√	
supply request			√	
visitor form (to be put in Care Team Director's box)			√	
H. Room				
maintain an appropriate teaching environment	√	√	√	√
communicate repairs/needs to department director	√	√		
maintain supplies	√	√	√	√

(continued)

TEACHER JOB DESCRIPTION

	LT	CT	TH	ST
I. Support Ministry Directors				
Pray for each one	√	√	√	√
1. Resource director				
requisition resources	√	√	√	√
return resources	√	√	√	√
reserve/check out equipment	√	√	√	√
requisition new purchases	√	√		
2. Training director				
communicate needs	√	√	√	√
review training information	√	√	√	√
3. Recruitment director				
give referrals	√	√	√	√
communicate needs for help	√	√		
communicate replacement needs	√	√		
4. Promotions director				
give information about upcoming events	√	√		
communicate ideas	√	√		
support promotions in classroom	√	√	√	√

Christian Education Handbook

+ + + + + + +

A Christian Education Handbook is one of the most important tools to have available for every volunteer. The investment of time and money will provide a guide for reaching the goals established by the vision. Volunteers will be supported and encouraged by the information made available to them.

A handbook with five sections will be an effective tool. Of course, this is a suggestion. Tailor the handbook to your specific program.

Part One—Mission Statement and Goals

In this section include a statement of the long-range and short-range vision for your Christian education ministry. Include the goals that need to be accomplished to make that vision a reality. Include a mission statement. Scripture that sets the tone for your ministry should also be included.

Part Two—Who Makes It Happen

Begin by naming the members of the Christian education ministry team. Include addresses and phone numbers. This information will invite volunteers to communicate with them. Follow with a listing of directors/coordinators. Again, include phone numbers. If volunteers have access to a church directory, addresses may not be necessary. Include e-mail addresses for the convenience of those who choose the convenience and speed of e-mail.

The next section needs to provide names and phone numbers of all volunteers arranged by program. Include Sunday school, church time, choirs, clubs, etc. List classes in order of ages/grades. Include room numbers or other location designation.

Part Three—How Do We Do It?

Anything related to methods/techniques of teaching should be included in this section. Here is a list of possible topics to include.

1. Age/grade level characteristics
2. Ways students learn
3. Information about curriculum

4. Methods of lesson planning

5. How to increase learning with guided conversation

6. How to lead a discussion

7. Involving learners in meaningful activities

8. Building relationships with learners

Check the teacher enrichment session plans at the end of this book for some help with these topics. Be aware of reproducible resources with information that will help volunteers with methods and skills. Make copies and ask volunteers to add them to the handbook.

Part Four—Policies and Procedures

Nothing is more frustrating or unsettling for volunteers than to be in a situation and not know what is expected. Policies and procedures must be clearly written, read initially when becoming a part of the teaching ministry, reviewed as needed, and updated when changes occur. This is another part of the handbook that must be developed for each church. However, here is a list of things to include for your consideration. It would seem that they are all necessary and you may be aware of others you wish to include.

1. Discipline Policy—What do you want volunteers to do when all reasonable efforts have been made to change behavior without positive results? Do they contact the director? Do they contact the parent? Establish clear guidelines to be followed when usual methods to bring about acceptable behavior choices fail.

2. Baby Care Guidelines—Who may check in or pick up a baby? What kind of identification will be used? What are diaper changing procedures? What are guidelines for cleaning linens, cribs, toys, etc.

3. What are adult to learner ratios? The general rule is one adult for the number of years old for young children. That is, one adult for every 3 three-year-olds, etc. One adult for every 6 to 8 elementary children. One adult for every 10 teens. One teacher for every 25 adults. If adult classes are larger, there are usually small groups of 8 to 10 for building relationships and ministry purposes. There must always be at least two adults with every group of children and teens. The abuse issue is one that cannot be ignored by churches—for protection of both learners and adult volunteers. It is important to check with your church insurance provider to determine the requirements for ratio of adults to children and teens. There may requirements to be sure that negligence is not a possibility.

4. How are volunteers expected to handle concerns? Include a list of doctors, nurses, and CPR-trained members and their locations during various times classes are in session. Provide a first aid kit for every classroom. Include health and allergy information on all registration forms so that teachers will be aware of precautions related to the well-being of students.

5. What procedures are in place for volunteers to follow when they plan to provide an activity or field trip outside of the classroom? What permission slips must be completed? How is transportation to be arranged? What are some suggested activities? Be sure that these procedures are well established and clearly communicated.

Support Volunteers

+ + + + + + +

Make a commitment to support all volunteers. Perhaps one of the greatest factors in poor volunteer retention is the lack of support volunteers often face. There are many different forms of support, each of which is important to the well-being and spiritual development of your volunteers.

1. The most important support is prayer support. The Christian education ministry team ought to pray for directors and coordinators. Coordinators should pray for teachers. Teachers should pray for learners. Enlist prayer volunteers in addition to those directly involved in the teaching ministry.

2. Know reasons volunteers drop out of the teaching ministry. Then provide the support needed to prevent the drop out. If the curriculum doesn't work, train and help teachers to use the curriculum. If there is not enough time to prepare, provide additional volunteers who will help to prepare materials. If resources are lacking, provide necessary resources.

3. Be sure the budget is adequate. Be frugal, but provide necessary tools.

4. People tools are most important. Effective learning situations just do not happen if the number of adults is not adequate. RECRUIT, RECRUIT, RECRUIT until there are enough workers in every class of every program.

5. Provide the best facilities possible. New classrooms that include all of the suggested characteristics are not always available. You may be years and years away from a building program. Evaluate existing facilities. Will new paint help? Will moving classes to different rooms that better accommodate the number of learners help? What will a thorough cleaning do

to help the classroom environment? Much can be done to make better use of existing facilities. Never stop evaluating and trying to improve, one realistic step at a time.

6. Is it possible to provide a resource room? Study curriculum to see what resources are needed. Be sure the resource room is well maintained. All too frequently it becomes a storage space, greatly lacking in resources and organization. Survey volunteers to ascertain the supplies and equipment they would like to use. Include as many resources as possible in the resource room.

Provide Encouragement

+ + + + + + +

Consider the words of Paul in 1 Thessalonians 5:11: "Therefore encourage one another and build each other up, just as in fact you are doing." One of the greatest encouragements for volunteers is evidence of spiritual growth in their own lives. Be sure every volunteer has opportunity for Bible study and encouragement to grow spiritually. Teams of volunteers can provide encouragement for each other. They all need to be part of a small group that is organized with encouragement, spiritual growth, and building up of each other as goals. Keep spiritual growth at the forefront of thinking of volunteers. They are each valuable and important to God. He desires his best for them. Be sure this is reinforced.

Recruitment and Accountability

+ + + + + + +

Regular, specific affirmation is an important part of encouragement for volunteers. Chapter 6 provides many ideas for affirmation that will be appreciated by your volunteers.

Continuous motivation that involves changes of hearts, attitudes, and minds is part of supporting and retaining volunteers. Change is not easy. Hurry slowly! People need time to accept and take ownership of change. This is an all important part of motivation. See chapter 5 for motivation specifics.

There must be a plan for accountability built into the recruitment process. Perhaps the job description is a starting point. Behaviors and items that are expected must be part of the job description. It is not realistic to expect a behavior if the volunteer does not know it is expected.

For example, if volunteers are expected to participate in teacher enrichment sessions, that must be stated in the job description. If teachers are expected to arrive in the classroom twenty minutes before the beginning of the session, that must be part of the job description.

Regular participation in worship should be an expectation. Investing time in building relationships with learners may be an expectation. When the expectations are clearly communicated, the next step is to plan for regular accountability checks. Make it possible for any volunteer to seek out a team member or director to question or discuss concerns at any time. In addition to that, consider the following suggestions. Adapt the suggestions to meet the goals and needs of your church.

1. Plan for an evaluation conversation after the volunteer has been involved for one month. Be prepared to affirm strengths you have observed and to offer support for any struggles. Respond to questions and concerns of the volunteer.

2. Arrange an appointment for a quarterly review. Ask such questions as What do you enjoy about your teaching ministry? How can I support you as you serve? What are three things you are doing well? What is one thing we could help you with? You may wish to ask the volunteer to prepare a list of items he wishes to discuss. An annual review during late spring or summer will keep the recruiting director/team aware of the need for additional volunteers and also of ways to continue to support and encourage the current volunteers.

God Will Provide!

+ + + + + + +

Be encouraged by the words of Jesus in Matthew 9:37, 38. "The harvest is plentiful but the workers are few. Ask the Lord of the harvest, therefore, to send out workers into his harvest field." It is his harvest field! It is his teaching ministry. They are his volunteers. Pray that he will use recruiters and their strategy so that the harvest may be gathered. God will provide teachers!

GOD SEND US TEACHERS

A little child in Sunday school,
A heart for God to touch
Through crafts and Bible stories
And songs and games and such.
A life to lead to Jesus,
Small hands to guide with love,
Small feet to show his pathway
With guidance from above.
Small lips to tell his praises,
Small hearts to know his joy—
Dear God, just send a teacher
To love that girl or boy.

A teen who's scared and hurting
Whose doubts scream in his head,
Whose heart is near to breaking;
Each day brings fear and dread.
He just needs some dear someone
To show him God is real,
Someone to show him Jesus,
His fear and pain to heal.
Dear God, just send a teacher
Who'll gladly bear the cost,
To lead that teen to Jesus
Who's hurt and scared and lost.

A mom and dad in Sunday school,
A smile stuck on their face.
But their home is broke and crumbling:
They are losing in life's race.
Dear God, just send a teacher
Who can see beyond the smile,
Who can feel the pain and anguish
And walk them down each mile.

Dear God, we just need teachers
Who can love the way You do.
Who can lead the way to Jesus,
Who can show Your Word is true.
Give us teachers fully committed
To take the time to do it right—
Who You can use to lead Your children
Through Your Word to win the fight.

And Lord, we thank You for our teachers,
Those who give their all to You.
Bless their class time every Sunday,
And bless each loving thing they do.
Bless the teachers with Your presence,
Let Your wisdom guide each day.
Bless the teachers' every effort
As they plan and teach and pray.

Chapter Three

Training and Enriching Volunteers for Service

Mary was a new volunteer Sunday school teacher. She had been teaching only a few weeks and already was frustrated, harboring feelings of failure and despair. Her biggest frustration was with the curriculum her church was using. There was just too much material, and she could never get through it all in any given class time.

Mary heard about a Sunday school convention in her area, and out of desperation, she decided to attend, hoping for help for her dilemma. When she got to the convention, Mary discovered that the curriculum publisher had an exhibit and a representative there. Mary approached him and explained her frustration wiht the curriculum. "It's either really bad material, or I'm a terrible teacher," she sighed.

The publisher's representative then took the time to show her that neither was true. He found the teacher's book for her age-level and walked her through a lesson. He showed that she didn't have to use all the material, that there were options she could choose for her own students.

As a smile eased itself across Mary's face and a tear ran down her cheek, Mary exclaimed, "Then I'm not a failure, am I?"

How many Marys walk the halls of your Sunday school department? How many teach each week having received no training? With just a little attention from a curriculum publisher's representative, a light came on for Mary. For many others, the light never comes on.

you and identifies you in that role. In the classroom it's a different story. It's possible to go weeks and months without a lot of interaction. This underscores the value of building a team.

To strengthen fellowship, it's important to include opportunity to enjoy being together when you meet. A game, sharing of testimonies, refreshments, etc. contribute to this purpose. Keep the schedule moving, but allow some time for people to enjoy being together.

These five characteristics of good training are most effective when you are able to have a regular training schedule. A football team continues training throughout the season. To be effective on the field requires regular times with the coaching staff. In the teaching ministry the same commitment to training helps build confidence, creates a higher level of enthusiasm, and improves teaching skills. Teaching 3rd and 4th graders is not a life sentence in solitary confinement. It is a matter of helping students come into a personal relationship with Jesus Christ and grow as his children.

Planning for Training

+ + + + + + +

Many times training just doesn't happen in churches simply because it isn't planned. A common adage in the business world is "plan the work, then work the plan." If you want to implement an effective training program, plan for it. When it comes to getting your volunteers involved in the plans, schedule training when it works best for your people, which may not necessarily be your preference. Consider these options:

• Strict, regular meetings (one Sunday or weeknight every month, every six weeks, or once a quarter)

• During Sunday school once a quarter with parent volunteers and others to cover the classrooms

• A short session may work on Sunday morning by having parent helpers come in 10 to 15 minutes before the end of Sunday school. Then you can meet with teachers for 20 to 25 minutes prior to the worship service. (Adapt this idea to fit your Sunday morning schedule.)

• Smaller departmental training can be scheduled on any day and at any time that works for those involved.

• Consider the possibility of piggybacking on other events at the church to minimize travel, to minimize the need for the child care, and to minimize additional commitments.

However, be careful not to reduce the effectiveness of other programs by requiring your volunteers to attend such "parallel" training sessions.

Using a combination of some of these scheduling ideas will help you have a better percentage of teacher involvement. Your goal should be to get maximum participation throughout the year. But keep in mind that not everyone can attend every session.

Conventional Training Ideas

+ + + + + + +

Training isn't a foreign concept to most people. Even people who are not deeply involved in our increasingly pervasive corporate culture are familiar with "conventional training." Conventional training refers to meetings and sessions where everyone involved knows that the purpose of the meeting is to give information that will help them do their job better.

Regular Meetings

The "bread and butter" of a good teacher training program will be meetings of the staff for encouraging, equipping, energizing, and empowering. Church leaders need to view training as an on-going process to ensure vitality and freshness for the entire staff. The development of new classroom skills and methods should be the highlight of these events for the inexperienced and experienced alike.

For these training meetings to be effective, they must provide practical helps that are presented in an attractive way. Keep in mind this wise twenty-first century proverb: "Nothing lasts as long as a box of cereal you don't like and a training session you can't stand." So, how do you make training events both effective and attractive?

First, people are willing to sacrifice time and energy for such events when they know it will be worth their time. You don't want them to attend your training session and then wonder what you were talking about for an hour and twenty minutes and why they were there in the first place. Therefore, your program needs to be practical enough that by the end of the session each person who has attended has found at least one idea to put into practice almost immediately.

Second, good promotion and publicity will attract interest. The leader needs to create a sense of expectation on the part of all participants. You can build that sense of expectation by promoting training events in the various communication mediums your church uses. Promote through the church bulletin and newsletter. Send reminder cards. Use e-mail. Provide a calendar for the year highlighting the topics to be covered (see the sample on page 60).

Third, be sure to provide variety in your sessions. Use instructional videos or Microsoft Power Point presentations. Invite guest workshop leaders or use panel discussions featuring your church's experts or experts from other churches or even curriculum publishing companies. Occasionally you may want to use people from within your teaching staff or from the congregation at large to make use of their special skills, interests, or experiences.

Hands-On Training

Include experiential involvement. As participants observe and practice new skills, they develop confidence. For example, if you are trying to help teachers of preschoolers be more effective with block building, puzzles, etc., let the teachers play with blocks or puzzles and have them experience what their students experience first-hand. Of course, you don't want to have an adult "free-play time," so have the participants evaluate their experiences and discuss them through guided conversation.

Periodically do live demonstrations of particular age-level concepts and methods using classroom experiences with children and experienced teachers. Many concepts can be clarified as you allow participants to observe in a demonstration setting. This method can help teachers make the best use of curriculum, develop guided conversation skills, and introduce new classroom procedures. Model good teaching skills in your training sessions. Your teachers will go out to teach as you have shown them, not simply as you have told them.

You can also build sessions around specific themes. Decorate the room accordingly, using a variety of room arrangements. When the participants enter the room and find that it is not the typical classroom, their expectations of what the training session will bring will increase. You can also change the perception of the classroom in your teachers' minds and greatly increase their creativity, fueling them for greater impact in their own classrooms.

Planning Sessions

Once you've presented your information, make sure that it is applied by allowing some time for departmental planning. Give the participants time to make plans for implementing their training while it is fresh in their minds, while their creative juices are still brewing. Jealously guard your schedule to make sure that planning is not eased out. A team that works together needs to plan together.

Area Seminars, Conferences, and Conventions

+ + + + + + +

Publishing houses, denominational groups, Sunday school conventions, and other educational conferences provide training events that are helpful. Many will include practical training that is not easily available at the local church level. One of the benefits of these events is the opportunity to interact with people from a variety of churches who minister in a given age level. Networking and sharing ideas with others is also a great encouragement to one's own ministry.

Sunday school conventions and other large events offer a smorgasbord of workshops and seminars. You might want to peruse the program in advance and highlight the sessions that you believe to be most appropriate for your people. By highlighting these you can help them choose wisely. When two or more people from a church attend a conference, it is often thought to be more efficient to have each person attend different sessions. Then after the conference, individuals can share the information from their sessions so that the whole group will benefit. Discuss how things learned in the sessions could best be applied or adapted in your setting.

As a leader you are responsible to evaluate any of these events and encourage the participation of all workers who would benefit. Churches that value such training often include in their budgets funds for covering all or part of the cost of attendance. This is why it is important for the leader to investigate upcoming events and try to plan accordingly.

Unconventional Training

+ + + + + + +

Just as the students your teachers teach have different learning styles and modes, so do your teachers and volunteers. While most people recognize and expect "conventional" training in most church volunteer programs, there are people who simply do not respond well to having regular meetings and training sessions. And even those people who do like regular training and planning meetings may find some of the following ideas of "unconventional training" appealing. Try to take advantage of varied learning styles, mediums, and events to ensure that your entire staff benefits from training efforts.

Practical and Fun Meetings

This year we have scheduled teacher enrichment sessions to continue our commitment to excellence in Bible teaching. And we are making it easier than ever for you to be a part of these important get-togethers. You'll get a reminder in the mail prior to each meeting asking you to RSVP. You'll not want to miss these great sessions with "your partners in ministry."

Our schedule is to meet on Sundays at 12:15 in Fellowship Hall. Please mark your calendars now.

12:15 p.m.—Lunch for you and your family

12:45 p.m.—Child care in our Education Building

12:45 p.m.—Teacher Training & Department Planning

2:00 p.m.—Dismiss

Not to be Missed!

The calendar for this year is:

August 27—Some Things Old, Some Things New—We Have a Great Year Planned!

September 17—Our Curriculum Is Not a Strait Jacket (special guest speaker)

October 15—Creative Activities to Make Bible Learning Fun

November 19—Helping Children Learn to Pray

December 10—Family Christmas Celebration

January 14—21 Super Ideas You Can Begin Using Next Week!

February 25—Discipline Need Not be a Problem

March 25—Easter Activities for Your Classroom

April 29—What Has God Done This Year?

Come expecting great things to happen as we allow the Holy Spirit to work through us.

Training Workshop Tips

+ + + + + + +

First, have an event not a meeting. Calling meetings often gives people the impression of a business function or some other unappealing task. One way to reduce the negative images of having a meeting is to give it a greater perceived value and make it festive! Find out what your volunteers want or need and give it to them. Promise them fun (and deliver it).

Second, start each session right. Remember, the first seven seconds of your presentation sets the stage for attracting and holding the participants' attention and interest. Avoid such beginnings as, "Our topic tonight is..." or "As we suggested last month...." Start right off with something that will capture their attention and go from there. The first impression the group gets of you can make or break your workshop. To create an opening that will ensure interest, try one of these:

- A rhetorical question such as "Have you ever..." or "Remember when...."
- Ask a question that calls for a show of hands.
- State a simple fact.
- Tell an appropriate story that fits your theme.
- Make a startling statement—a shocker to gain attention.
- Show a cartoon or other visual. Sometimes a brief video clip with little or no introduction will set the stage.
- Involve the group in an ice-breaker activity that's fun and engrossing and that will make transition into your presentation natural.

Third, keep in mind that ice breakers are not just for cold groups. It's true that ice breakers are helpful in getting strangers to know each other. But they also can help in your training sessions by

- energizing people who've come to the meeting after a long, hard day or week;
- building team spirit;
- helping those who already know each other get better acquainted; and
- focusing attendees on the theme or goal for the session.

Fourth, position yourself carefully. Imagine that you're leading a training session and have asked a question and a participant offers a comment. It's natural to step toward the person as you listen, but it's also mistake. In a group setting, respondents tend to speak as if the trainer is their only audience. Moving closer prompts them to speak softer—and they can become totally inaudible to those seated farthest away. What's the solution? Slowly back away from responding participants, being careful to maintain eye contact. The speaker will usually increase his or her volume to adjust for the distance—and everyone will be able to hear.

16 Sizzling Ideas for Workshop Activities

✝ ✝ ✝ ✝ ✝ ✝ ✝

Few volunteers would suggest that the classes they teach or groups that they lead should focus solely on lecture or any single type of presentation. Why should your training workshops be any different? If you can model active learning in your training sessions, you will most likely find your volunteers using active teaching methods in their classes. Try a few of these ideas.

1. Nails, Needles and Nuisance

Before your training session set up three activity centers with an instruction card at each center. As participants arrive, direct them to choose from among several projects to complete.

The first center, "Nails," contains a block of wood and three-penny nails which are to be hammered into the wood using a plastic ruler.

At the second center, "Needles," participants are to thread a small-eyed needle while wearing a pair of ski gloves.

The third center, "Nuisance," is a block of wood with a Phillips head screw in it, which is to be removed using snub-nosed pliers.

As they work, make note of each participant's progress and make appropriate comments, such as, "the nail is bent," or "that thread really doesn't want to go in, does it?" After several minutes of discussion or possible frustration, transition into a discussion of why having and using the right tools is critical to an effective teaching ministry. This activity can be used to introduce a variety of sessions and can be tailored to fit the appropriate occasions.

2. Wire Sculpture

Give each person a chenille wire (pipe cleaner) or a "twist tie" (the papered wires used in grocery stores to tie up bags of produce) and ask participants to bend the wire into some shape that represents the idea of caring for learners and their families. Encourage them not to worry about being creative and clever—just do whatever comes to mind first. (Paper tearing would also work for this idea.)

3. Paper Clips Are More Than They Appear

In any session where creative thinking is pivotal, provide each person with a jumbo paper clip and ask the group what this "tool" is for and how it is used. After a general consensus is reached on these points, suggest that there may be many other uses for paper clips. You may divide the class into small groups and ask each group to spend three minutes listing other uses for paper clips.

Instruct the groups to take turns sharing their ideas. In most cases the creativity will be incredible. The message is clear: We sometimes let what we "know" keep us from accepting or creating new ideas. If we set aside what we know, it opens our mind to new learning.

4. Three Coins

Ask each person in a small group to take one, two, or three coins from her pocket or purse. Each person then introduces himself or herself to the group by relating an important personal or ministry related event that occurred in the year imprinted on the coin. This is a good activity at the beginning of the year when there are new teachers coming on board. This activity also works well to introduce a session on an appropriate topic with people who know each other.

5. Using Blocks

Here's a simple and economical idea for getting better acquainted with others in a group. You'll need one child's wooden block per participant and a bag for the blocks.

Put the blocks in the bag and have each person take one. Participants then introduce themselves using one of the symbols on their blocks. Each person has six choices—letters, numbers, shapes, or symbols on each face of his block.

Participants may use as many faces on their blocks as they wish—from one to six. Shy participants may choose to talk briefly about one letter, number, or symbol. Others may use all six and give lots of information about themselves. Everyone will enjoy thinking of creative things to share!

6. Using Pictures

Pictures make excellent learning and review tools for teacher training sessions. Photos and slides of actual or staged classroom situations do a great job illustrating key points or techniques, such as discipline, learning centers, visuals, learning activities, and more.

13. The AHA! Factor

Before you start the session, distribute note cards with "AHA!" written at the top of each one. Instruct your volunteers to write down any great ideas they discover in the training time—from you, from other attendees, or from audio visuals. These should be ideas that could help them be more effective in ministry. When the session needs a change of pace, invite people to share any "Ahas" they've written on their cards.

14. License Plate

Use this activity at your first training session of the season when you have new volunteers who have just joined the team. Give each person a form designed in the likeness of a blank license plate. Ask the group to create their own personalized plates, using no more than seven letters or numbers.

When they have completed their license plates, ask participants to introduce themselves to the rest of the group using their new "vanity" plate as a starting point. Instruct each participant to allow the group a few moments to decode the plate before explaining it, as some will probably be quite tricky.

Some samples might be SNGLMM (single mom); DADOV4 (dad of four); SWMITR (swimming instructor); 3GR7YR (taught 3rd grade for 7 years).

15. To Tell the Truth

Invite four or five attendees to come to the front of the room. Give each a note card and ask them to write four statements about themselves, three to be true and one false. Have each of the volunteers read their statements to the entire group. The rest of the group must then try to determine which statement is wrong. After a few minutes of this, move into your training by indicating how important it is that they teach God's Word with integrity and excellence.

16. Maximize Videos

When using videos, never leave a group watching a videotape on their own. If it's important enough for them to see, it's important for you to see it with them and observe how they are responding to it.

Consider dividing participants into observation teams. Give each team something different to watch for while viewing the video. After viewing, give them time to discuss their findings within the team. Finally, ask each team to give a group report on what they have discussed. Plan for creative ways to do the reporting—role-play, visuals, music, etc.

You can get triple duty (or more) from every training video by using each one in a variety of ways, such as:

• Short clips—select three- to five-minute clips from longer tapes to illustrate specific topics.

• Follow-up—include the same video, in its entirety, in your resource center, and code it for easy topic cataloging.

• Self-study—use the video as part of a self-study program, providing a viewing guide with specific things to look for as volunteers view it.

Chapter Four

Discipling Volunteers by Building Relationships

It was about 10:00 a.m. on a bright sunny spring day when Eric got the phone call from Ed, who offered to buy his lunch. Not one to turn down a free meal, especially from a good friend and member of his Sunday school class, Eric eagerly accepted the invitation. Ed promised to pick Eric up at noon, and Ed was always prompt.

Although Eric had been in Ed's home many times and had hosted Ed and his family often, as well, he began to wonder about the invitation. Ed was a successful businessman, husband to a wonderful wife, and father of three teenagers, who almost never had the time for a leisurely lunch. Eric, however, chalked the invitation up to a warm and shared friendship and began to look forward to the appointment.

It was after they had finished the meal and shared some pleasant conversation that Ed revealed the real purpose of the lunch invitation when he shocked Eric by saying, "I'm going to tell you something I haven't told to another soul, including my wife." Ed continued, "I'm going home this afternoon and ask Mary for a divorce. I don't love her anymore."

For a brief moment Eric was caught off guard and struggled for the right words to say. He knew Ed and Mary had been married for 28 years and certainly thought their relationship was good.

Over the next couple of months Eric talked and prayed with Ed and Mary. There were many tears of pain and anguish shed, and

confidential conversations. They need to be sensitive to needs. Actually these qualities should be part of every believers life as they relate to others. Living out the "One Anothers" of Scripture will enable us to live so that relationships are a joyous part of our ministry (see page 142).

5. Opportunities to express needs help to build relationships.

Develop a plan that allows volunteers to share their needs. Provide a basket with slips of paper for volunteers to write needs/prayer requests. Remember the words of Galatians 6:2, "Carry each others' burdens." Share and pray together face to face or with a phone call. Organize a prayer chain.

6. Provide caring experiences.

Availability is a key word. Never be too busy to express a caring attitude. Again, focus on a reasonable number of volunteers. Involve others in the ministry of caring. Work together. Pray together. Organize a "secret pal" or "buddy" plan. Letters, notes, cards, and phone calls are all ways to communicate caring that do not require a large investment of time and yet clearly say, "I am praying for you. I care about you."

Sensitivity to Special Needs

+ + + + + + +

Volunteers in the teaching ministry are usually recruited to serve for a period of one year. Many choose to continue for additional years. Some ask to be replaced at the end of their commitment for one year. In either case, we can be sure that some volunteers will need to deal with unexpected special needs. Be sensitive to those special needs. Surround your volunteers and their families with care and concern. Meet those needs that you can meet. Always support with diligence.

Building relationships not only requires an investment of time. It also requires a servant attitude. It requires a willingness to go the extra mile to meet unexpected and unusual needs. One of the most obvious special needs would be illness. The volunteer may become ill and need to be replaced, even for an extended period of time. Be sure that the teaching team and substitutes are ready to assume this responsibility without difficulty. A family member may become ill, causing stress and additional tasks for the volunteer. Be ready to provide a substitute if necessary. Perhaps you need to create a plan that allows some of the tasks to be performed by others in the church family.

Sometimes the special need is beyond the tasks of a volunteer's ministry. Perhaps in addition to finding a substitute to cover a sick volunteer's teaching responsibilities, there may be a need for help at the volunteer's home. In many churches there is a ministry team prepared to provide meals; if not, you may need to mobilize your team to do so. Sometimes help with child care is needed. Help with transportation may be needed. It may be helpful to care for laundry, grocery shopping, or any of dozens of tasks that require time and energy. Whatever the need may be, if you can provide for it or at least help a volunteer deal with the need, you will strengthen the relationship you have with that person.

Share Dreams and Goals

+ + + + + + +

Sharing dreams and goals helps to build and strengthen relationships. Chapter 1 provides many suggestions for sharing ministry vision and goals. Building relationships requires some sharing of personal dreams and goals. Know workers well enough to discuss and help set personal goals. Goals for spiritual growth are most important. Goals for children should be included. Goals for increasing teaching skills may be discussed. Relationships are strengthened when people share as many areas of their lives as possible.

Build Relationships with the Entire Church Family

+ + + + + + +

The entire church family is an important part of the education program of our churches. Building relationships between the Christian education ministry team and the entire congregation is essential. We have already discussed involvement in prayer, involvement in support roles, and ways to continuously build congregational awareness. Here are a few suggestions of ways to increase and build on congregational awareness which will, in turn, strengthen relationships with and ownership in the ministry.

Christian Education Ministry Fair

Begin to plan for a ministry fair at least six months before the date. Be sure that every education ministry is represented. The fair should supply information, opportunity for fellowship, and should be a fun activity.

Let's begin with the nursery ministry. Display pictures of babies in the nursery. Tell one special fact about each infant. Provide a guessing game (how many diapers are changed on Sunday morning?). The winner is given a disposable diaper and the opportunity to work in the nursery one Sunday morning. Provide baby-size dolls and disposable diapers and then time how long it takes a person to change a diaper. The fastest changer wins the opportunity of working in the nursery for one session. Include a sign-up sheet for additional nursery volunteers.

Provide opportunities for adults to participate with children in preschool and elementary classes. Set up activities that would be done in a typical lesson. Include Bible learning activities. Plan for some Bible memory games. Provide video recordings of a variety of classes in action. Involve children and adults in music activities. The possibilities are endless.

Encourage teens to share important parts of their ministry program. Again, get adults involved in typical activities with their teens. Include opportunities to experience service projects or ways to reach out into the neighborhood.

Adult teachers and students will be able to plan for ways to share information about their classes. Share the number of available classes. Inform everyone of the topics being studied. Are there elective classes that people can take instead of the class they normally attend? Are there studies where the focus is on specific books of the Bible? Share information about small groups ministry. Let people know what classes do to reach out to others. What kind of involvement does each class have in missions work?

A ministry fair requires time, planning, and effort. It can become a very exciting annual event. Informative and fun are two strong components of relationship building. The words of Ephesians 4:25-32 provide some guidelines for attitudes and actions that contribute to strong relationships.

1. Speak the truth.
2. Share.
3. Be kind and compassionate.
4. Forgive each other.
5. Build others up.

Develop a "ministry of loving surprises." Jesus' words in John 13:34, 35 tell us exactly how to do this. "A new command I give you: Love one another. As I have loved you, so you must love one another. By this all men will know that you are my disciples, if you love one another."

Chapter Five

Motivating Volunteers to Excellence

As a seventeen-year-old high school senior, Seth had taught his second- and third-grade Sunday school class for almost two years. In the spring of his seventeenth year, Seth graduated from a local Phoenix, Arizona, high school and was looking forward to the fall and his trek off to college and the new adventure of dorm life on his own.

As August approached, Seth began to realize just how much he was going to miss this class of children he had grown to love. With some reluctance Seth went to class on his last day as "Mr. Seth," Sunday school teacher, and with mixed emotions taught the lesson he had prepared, wondering in his own mind if he had made any difference in the lives of those children.

The lesson ended. Seth was preparing to leave the room when it happened. She approached him rather timidly and handed him a box, gift-wrapped with all the expertise of a third grader. In the corner of her eye was the trace of a tear. Seth self-consciously accepted the box and began the task of unwrapping it when that precious little child rather apologetically exclaimed, "Oh, don't open it Mr. Seth—it doesn't have anything in it but my love."

Seth turned away with tears welling up in his eyes, and at that moment "Mr. Seth" knew the joy of ministry and realized the value of being a volunteer teacher. Mr. Seth had certainly made a difference in at least one child's life.

Motivating Volunteers

+ + + + + + +

Motivation comes in various forms, many of which we have no control over. There is, however, much we can and must do to keep our volunteers motivated. As has been previously stated, perhaps the most difficult task you have as a ministry leader is to keep your volunteer staff motivated.

In a real sense this entire book is about motivation. Recruiting people to excellence is, in reality, a strong motivation, as excellence by its very nature is motivational. Good training of your volunteers is good motivation. When people feel competent in what they do, they are motivated to continue in that endeavor. Building relationships is clearly a strong motivation. People are often personally motivated when they feel loved and cared for. Constant and positive encouragement is powerful motivation. Ministries have risen and fallen by strong encouragement or the lack thereof. Open and continuous appreciation is certainly an incredible way to motivate people. Someone has said, "If you want more Christian education workers, make heroes out of the ones you have." Each of these chapters has a great deal to do with motivation. Still, there are other areas and ways to motivate our volunteers that need to be explored.

Set Goals

+ + + + + + +

In the first chapter of this book we talked about ministry goals and how essential they are for our ministries to be successful. Just as it is crucial that we set goals for our ministries, it is vital that we set goals for our volunteer workers.

What difference will it make in the lives of your volunteers that they are a part of your ministry team? What difference will it make in their spiritual life, in their personal life? Just as we want our teachers to make a difference in the lives of their students, so we must make a difference in the lives of our teachers. If it's not going to make a difference, then why should we expect them to commit to the ministry?

Set spiritual goals for your volunteers. Where should your fifth grade Sunday school teacher be in his or her walk with Jesus six months into the ministry? A year? Five years? This presupposes that you know where they are now in their spiritual walk. How do you know that?

That's easy—build relationships (see chapter 4). Building relationships is as much about time as commitment. However, if we truly desire to build a ministry of excellence, there are no short cuts.

Jesus taught us that there are only two truly important things in life—God and people. He came to demonstrate how to build relationships with both God and people. And he came to demonstrate how building relationships with God compels us—even requires us—to build better relationships with other people, and vice versa.

Some ministry structures make building relationships difficult, if not impossible. Structure your ministry in such a way that facilitates the building of relationships. If you have sixty volunteers, you obviously cannot adequately build relationships with each of them. Organize in departments or teams. Recruit people to be department heads or team leaders and start building relationships there. This way you can build relationships with six to ten department heads, or team leaders, who in turn will build relations with six to ten teachers. It's just the "Jesus model" in the local church ministry. After all, if Jesus, who is God's very Son, built relationships with only twelve disciples in order to start the church, who are we to think we can do better?

Once your structure is manageable, then it becomes much easier to set goals. When you work to set goals with six to ten to twelve individuals, you can focus on personal needs and set up realistic accountability. Help them set goals for their prayer life development, their personal Bible study time, and their devotional lives. If you are not seeing real spiritual growth in your ministry team, then something is amiss, and your ministry will never be all it can be.

Set personal goals for your volunteers. Dedicated servants involved in a God-given ministry will become better husbands, wives, parents, children, business people, etc. Obviously, you can't separate these entirely from their spiritual goals. If people have steadfast prayer lives and are committed to studying the word of God, then obviously their home lives will be affected. Their business lives will be affected.

Personal goals also extend to the area of ministry skills. A Sunday school teacher who is a good storyteller knows how to develop an exciting lesson, and can manage classroom behavior well, will certainly be a more motivated teacher. It should not surprise us that teachers with good skills feel better about teaching and will want to continue in a ministry in which they feel successful. Make it a matter of priority to assist your volunteers in identifying the skills necessary for their ministry area and developing those skills to greater levels of excellence.

Setting goals for your volunteers without holding them accountable to those goals makes the goals worthless. Where there is no accountability, there is no responsibility. It is not uncommon to hear someone say, "We can't hold them accountable—they are volunteers."

To fail to hold our volunteers accountable is to fail our volunteers. Paul wrote in 1 Thessalonians 5:12, 13, "Now we ask you, brothers, to respect those who work hard among you, who are over you in the Lord and who admonish you. Hold them in the highest regard in love because of their work." When we are "over" someone in the Lord, we are expected to admonish him or her, to hold them accountable. Ezekiel 34:1-10 gives a powerful account of how God will deal with those who do not care for his flock—and we are all shepherds! You shepherd your volunteers, and they shepherd their classes, youth groups, small groups, and so on. This is serious business we are involved in.

When you recruit people, be sure they know that there will be an accountability process. The accountability process is not as difficult as it may seem. If you set a goal for your Sunday school teachers to pray for each of their students by name, don't feel guilty about calling them and simply asking, "Have you prayed for your students by name today?" If you want your volunteers to develop a daily personal devotional time, don't hesitate calling them from time to time and asking, "Have you had your personal time with God today?" If your volunteers expect accountability, then they won't feel intimidated when you call. Help your volunteers develop priorities in their ministries, as well as in their spiritual and personal lives, and don't let them off the hook. Failure on your part as ministry leader to develop accountability almost ensures failure among the team members.

Plan times when you will sit down with your volunteers one-on-one and together evaluate their ministries, as well as their personal and spiritual growth processes. It is also a good plan to do written evaluations of each volunteer and to discuss the evaluations together. If you never evaluate progress against goals, then you will be unable to determine whether the ministry is having any positive impact on the volunteers or the volunteers on the ministry. Remember that ministry is about each of us coming to maturity in Christ as the body of Christ "grows and builds itself up in love, as each part does its work" (Ephesians 4:16). We need to be sure that each part does its work.

Accountability not only enables you to evaluate growth and effectiveness, it also assures your volunteer team that you truly care about them and their ministries. When they know that you are doing all you can to assist them in becoming the best they can be, then they will be motivated to persevere in the ministry, realizing that they are a part of something significant and eternal.

Providing for Needs

+ + + + + + +

Just as setting goals and holding your team of volunteers accountable for progress in reaching those goals is important, so is providing for the needs of your team. Possibly the most common reason people give for quitting a ministry team is burn out. Burn out, however, is foreign to the Bible. It is not a Biblical concept. No one in the Bible ever burned out. It is true that several people in the Bible burned up, but no one ever burned out.

Elijah, perhaps, came as close to burnout as anyone, but his real problem was he felt alone, unsupported, and discouraged. When he discovered there were others on the "ministry team," he regained his purpose and zeal. When people cry "burnout" they usually are indicating that there is some unmet need in their personal lives, be it encouragement, support, recapturing vision, or a number of other possibilities.

If you have a volunteer teaching a first grade Sunday school class every Sunday, making it impossible for him to attend a Sunday morning Bible study himself, then you need to provide a time when he can spend time in Bible study with other believers. There is certainly a difference in Bible study to prepare a lesson for a class of first graders and studying the Word for personal growth.

Listen to your volunteers when they are discouraged or frustrated, and hear what they are really saying, to find out what their needs are. If you are meeting the needs of your team well—by developing personal caring relationships and supporting them in every way possible—then they certainly will not want to leave that ministry. You have become more to each other than just a group of volunteers involved in a common task. In a real sense you have become a family!

Another area in which you need to be sure you support your team is in prayer. Continually pray for and with your volunteers. Develop prayer partnerships among team members as well as a prayer chain where needs can be communicated to the entire team and a massive prayer effort can begin. Encourage parents in the church to pray for their children's teachers and leaders. Enlist prayer support from the church leadership (elders, pastors, etc.). Refer to chapter 2 for other ideas for developing prayer support for your volunteer team.

Be acutely aware of the personal needs of your team. If a team member becomes unemployed and she is not sure where the house payment will come from, or where money to buy groceries for the family will come from, her effectiveness in ministry may certainly become side-tracked. In chapter 1 we mentioned a church in central Illinois with a Sunday school class that grew from 60 people and peaked at 247. Several times during that growth experience members of the class made house payments, bought groceries, and helped with medical expenses of other class members. This is truly the body of Christ living out the love of Jesus. Several times there was an attempt to split the class, but no one would leave. Who would want to leave a group of people, a family, who had stood beside them, encouraged them, and supported them in times of great need? When your team begins to truly minister to each other's needs and stands by each other through times of trouble and in times of joy—you won't be able to drive them off with a stick! That kind of motivation lasts a lifetime!

Demonstrate Value to Ministry

✝ ✝ ✝ ✝ ✝ ✝ ✝

In chapter 7 you will find many excellent ideas about creative ways to show your team your appreciation. As we have already stated, appreciation is powerful motivation. Listed below are some tried and proven ways to motivate your volunteer team.

Formal Recognition

In the morning worship service, have the senior minister or pastor ask volunteers in certain areas (children's ministry, nursery, etc.) to stand and be recognized for their volunteer ministry efforts. Be sure to offer hearty and heartfelt applause. Do this in addition to any special recognition days and do it fairly often. When the senior minister takes the time and makes the effort to recognize volunteers on a "regular" day, not for a special occasion, it is a powerful statement about the importance of volunteers.

Volunteer Wall of Fame

Designate a wall or a bulletin board as a Volunteer Wall of Fame. This should be a place that has high traffic and high visibility, so that anyone who enters your church will be able to see how much you value your volunteers and their work. Picture all of your teachers with their families and describe the ways in which they minister. Make the display big and impressive.

Volunteer of the Week

While it's imperative to recognize all of your volunteers, it's an added measure of thankfulness to focus on individuals. Each week highlight one volunteer and the ministry she does. Give her special recognition—have her wear a flower or a badge. Recognize her in your church newsletter. Give her a special little gift. Do this every week and make sure you give special recognition to all of your volunteers.

Volunteer of the Month

In addition to focusing on a special volunteer each week, do the same thing each month. Display a photograph of the volunteer in a frame on your "Wall of Fame" in the center of other smaller photos of the volunteer in action. Have a big write-up in your church newsletter about their family, their work, and their interests.

Special Parking Space

Many churches designate special parking for visitors or other people with special needs and ask their members to save "preferred" parking spaces for these people. How nice would it be to designate a special parking space for the Volunteer of the Week or Month? This space should be the best parking space in the lot, as close as possible to the main entrance. Have a professionally lettered sign that says, "Volunteer of the Month," or whatever designation you use. It is ideal to have this available for your volunteer of the month. When he pulls into that space each week and when others see him get out of his vehicle, it gives a sense of importance and credibility to both the volunteer and the church members who see him. It just says to everyone that your volunteers are special people.

Volunteer Ministry Map

A few years ago the national sales manager for a major division of an automobile manufacturer had on the wall of his office a map of the entire United States with a map pin in each city where he had a dealership. Beside that pin was a photo of each dealer and his family. The sales manager sent birthday cards to all the children of the dealers, anniversary cards to married couples, Christmas cards, etc. Every day the sales manager went over to the wall and prayed for three or four of his dealers and their families by name.

Would it make a difference in your ministry if your volunteers walked into your office or home and saw a map of your community with a pin marking where they live and a picture of their family? Would it motivate them if their children got birthday cards from you as well as cards recognizing special days in their lives? Would it impact them knowing that each day you walked over to that map and prayed for them by name? I think we all know the answers to those questions. And that's motivation!

Build a Positive Ministry Image

Corporations spend lots of money to create recognition of their company among the people in their markets. They design eye-catching logos, produce memorable commercials and advertisements, and do many other things that help people know who the company is and feel good about the company. Even though we are not trying to increase sales and build a profitable organization, we are trying to help people recognize who the church is and feel good about what the church does. There are lots of ways to build an image, and actually all of the ideas in this book are important parts of that process. Here are some more suggestions:

- develop a ministry logo
- choose a name for your ministry
- create ministry wear for team members (shirts, smocks, badges, etc.)
- have coffee mugs, key chains, refrigerator magnets made with your logo on them
- develop a ministry brochure to include in new member packets
- have ministry recognition events (see additional ideas in chapter 7)

People are truly motivated when they feel what they are doing is significant and worthwhile. It adds purpose to their lives and gives them a sense of achievement.

One church in Alaska who actually put into practice the first five ideas listed above reported, "It has made all the difference in the way we do Christian education. We don't have to beg people to serve now, and once they join our team, they stay."

Highly motivated volunteers set the stage for a highly effective ministry and enable us to truly make a difference in our communities for the cause of Christ. Make the ministry of motivation your ministry and build an army of volunteers who are committed to ministry and who are there for the long haul!

Chapter Six

Encouraging Volunteers to Commitment

Mindy, a mother of two young children, eagerly responded to the Children's Ministry Director's invitation to join the teaching team in the four-year-old department. Her own Brett was in that group last year and loved it. And Amy, her three year old, would be in there next year. So Mindy saw this as an opportunity to make a difference in the lives of other children as well as her own.

Those first weeks, working with Tim and Jill, went well. They had been given teaching materials by Marie, the director, and things appeared to be OK. Several attempts were made by the team to get together and plan, but it seemed there were always conflicting schedules. Mindy tried reaching Marie to get more directions on how to handle the class, but they were never able to speak directly. Often Marie took several days to call back. It was discouraging.

So what began as a venture filled with eagerness and anticipation suddenly became a chore. Having almost no contact with Marie, little interaction with Tim and Jill, and no training left Mindy feeling alone. She found herself dreading to show up on Sunday morning, and she considered dropping out after only a few months, wondering if anyone would even miss her.

Encouragement Is a Responsibility for Leaders

✛ ✛ ✛ ✛ ✛ ✛ ✛

There are a lot of Mindys out there with similar stories. How do we cope with that kind of scenario? If you are in a role of leadership—director, superintendent, ministry leader—you have a responsibility to see that those entrusted to your care are equipped, motivated, and encouraged in their ministry,

Volunteers, like any other person in ministry, need encouragement. Some are lonely, some are discouraged at the lack of success, and others have had little or no training and receive only minimal support at best.

Training is very important, as was explained in chapter 3, and motivation goes a long way to keep a volunteer staff on track, but encouragement is a major source of satisfaction for those involved in ministry. Let's look at a few things you can do to encourage ministry fulfillment and productivity.

Build Trust

Teachers and other volunteer staff members need to know that you care about them as individuals. Build an open, sharing relationship environment. Let's face it, none of us is always on top of things—we all face discouragement, we all struggle with disappointments, and sometimes we just have to cope with difficult situations.

Be open about your own feelings and failings. Sharing your own vulnerability will help to foster trust. When a volunteer knows she can come to you with a concern because you care, you are building trust.

Communicate Availability

Most of us frequently find ourselves caught up in a frenzy of activity and the last thing we need is another interruption. Dave, a children's pastor of a dozen years, said to his senior pastor, somewhat sadly, "You know, my whole life I've been complaining that my work is constantly interrupted until I realized that my interruptions are my ministry."

Some interruptions are unavoidable, such as the teacher who calls at 7:15 Sunday morning with two sick children and no one to care for them. Nor can you avoid emergencies like a car accident, death of a loved one, or other special cases.

But these are the exceptions, not the rule. A teacher may need special help with a difficult child, additional resources for a unique lesson, advice for handling an awkward situation, or just a willing, listening ear. It's important to be available for these needs.

It's wise and appropriate to let your staff know when you are most available. You may have certain hours of the day when you will most likely be able to take a call. And you may have certain times that are not convenient—staff meeting, study hour, family time—except for emergencies. Assure your volunteers that they are a priority and you are open to interruptions.

Prompt response to a message from a teacher needs to be high priority. You don't know what may surface at the other end of the line, and you can't anticipate what has been going on in the life of that teacher today. His call may be coupled with a myriad of unrelated issues that only compound the situation. There's nothing worse than a volunteer thinking you don't care enough to return their call. Return messages ASAP!

Also, make productive use of today's technology—voice mail, e-mail, and other means of staying in touch. With the advances in communications technology, keeping in touch is easier than ever. While playing "phone tag" can become annoying, it's often better than not communicating at all. You can respond to e-mail messages as soon as you receive them, and you can be as detailed and clear as possible without having to catch the other person at their desk or at home.

Demonstrate Authenticity

Teachers will freely share their needs, hopes and frustrations with leaders only if those leaders are approachable as well as available. To be approachable is to be an honest, open, authentic human being.

Authenticity needs to become a way of life. The words "thank you" can never be worn out. Initially they may seem stiff or awkward, but eventually they will fit like a glove. Being ready to support others in special ways also demonstrates authenticity. If you are aware of a special need, offer a helping hand. Be a good listener. You will discover countless ways to be an encourager. It is a powerful thing to communicate "You're carrying a heavy load right now" to one who is struggling with the loss of a loved one or who is under heavy pressure at home or work.

Being sensitive to the non-verbal cues is also an important element. Even among Christians who have strong relationships, it's common to find people who do not want to share their burdens or needs, for whatever reason. If you have strong relationships with your volunteers, however, you are more likely to discern when they have unspoken needs by what they are not saying and how they are acting.

At the same time we must respect the other person's sensitivities. Even when we are able to figure out that a volunteer is having a problem in her personal life, she may refuse help. Sometimes it's just as helpful to back off for awhile. Don't leave her stranded, but don't smother her. Respecting her wishes to be left alone for awhile will make it that much easier for her to ask for help later.

It all boils down to this—be a real person. Phonies don't make it. As we develop a loving, caring relationship with each volunteer, we can truly demonstrate that we are real.

Enable Creative Solutions

In order to be approachable, it's important to overcome the temptation to act the part of an expert and the tendency of others to cast you as such. Instead take on the role of enabler.

An enabler is one who helps make it possible for others to discover creative solutions to the challenges and problems that confront them. The enabler sets the scene for learning by providing resources, processes, and input that will allow volunteers to discover their own answers.

When you, as ministry leader, introduce or describe yourself to teachers and others, make a distinction between the terms. Stress that you're willing and able to be an enabler rather than an expert. Explain, by virtue of your experience and education, that you expect to be a valuable resource for them as they learn. At the same time, underscore that you also expect to learn from them as they bring unique experiences to bear.

Perhaps the best way to model this is by recognizing the value of people and their experiences. It is far too easy to care more for the program than the people involved. So, when you can model genuine appreciation for each person's insight and experiences, you will have empowered or enabled them to become excellent in their ministry.

Support Them with Resources

A church that provides adequate resources to help volunteers in their ministries communicates that those volunteers are valued by the church. Anything you can do to minimize a teacher's "busy work" will allow more time and energy for real preparation for class and ministry in general.

Things can be valuable resources. Make sure that sufficient supplies for most learning activities are readily available and stored in a convenient location. Many churches have a specific room set aside for maintaining a stock of needed items. Some of these materials will be purchased, and others will be collected. Purchased items include paper, paints, pens, art supplies, glue, tape, etc. Collected items may include yarn, margarine tubs, fabric scraps, greeting cards, paper towel rolls, etc. Make sure you have a complete list on a reproducible request form.

Equipment is a valuable resource. Be sure to have cassette and CD players, overhead projectors, musical and rhythm instruments, a paper cutter, a copy machine, and whatever other equipment your ministry volunteers need—and budget allows—readily available and in good working condition. For equipment that is kept in an office there should be easily understood policies as to how it is to be used and when it will be available. Other items may need to be reserved ahead of time, and again, the policies need to be well known. Make it easy for your staff to have access to tools that will enhance their ministry.

Curriculum resources are essential for providing a wide range of helps for teachers. The Bible curriculum materials, along with supplementary helps, are the main resources. A variety of audiovisuals are valuable resources along with helps for drama, music, and play activities. Many churches keep a complete file on all materials available to strengthen Bible lessons.

Communication resources also support the volunteer staff. A centrally located bulletin board reserved for information for the staff helps assure that important announcements are kept current. Use your best creativity to keep the bulletin board attractive and up to date.

Many ministry leaders give their volunteers a quarterly or monthly calendar, detailing regular meetings and programs they are expected to be a part of. You can also highlight special events and have a place for looking ahead to future months. Events announced well in advance allow them to become a part of each volunteer's calendar. Dress up your calendar with fun clip art that is readily available in books, in computer programs, and on the Internet. There really is no shortage of creative resources available.

Creative use of projected announcements—such as with overhead projectors or Microsoft Power Point presentations—can be used effectively in the worship service to get the word out. Use e-mail to communicate with as many teachers as possible. Brainstorm unique ways to communicate in your setting.

People resources are extremely valuable. Lack of time is the reason most often given when a person discontinues their involvement in volunteer ministry. Those who work with children use lots of materials and visuals weekly. Often just preparing these materials can become overwhelming.

In order to help teachers deal with such problems, recruit another group of volunteers to meet regularly (weekly, monthly, quarterly—as appropriate) to prepare materials to be used by teachers. Before the beginning of the quarter the student materials can be punched out, cut, sorted and put in envelopes by lesson to be stored in the classroom, ready for use when the teacher arrives on Sunday. What a load has been lifted from the teacher's role, and what a delightful and satisfying experience for those who gave of their time and energy to prepare the materials. Many who do this have a deep commitment to the teaching ministry but for various reasons are unable to work in the classroom on Sunday or feel they are unqualified to teach. In this capacity, these volunteers are able to make a significant contribution to the ministry, as well as to individual teachers. (Be sure to honor these volunteers for this kind of "second mile ministry.")

Encouraging one another is a sound Scriptural principle that should be the foundation of every Christian life. Sometimes the Bible teaching ministry can be discouraging. What a joy to be able to encourage those who serve faithfully investing their lives in classroom ministry.

God has entrusted you with leading your team. It's a great privilege and it's an awesome responsibility. Lead that team with excellence and celebrate the joy of encouragement!

Chapter Seven

Building Up Volunteers with Appreciation

It's nearly 10:00 Sunday morning. As usual, Amy and Fran find themselves picking up after a busy class session with an active group of first and second graders. They've been doing this for almost three years. And they are tired and feeling dry on ideas for how to teach these youngsters in fresh ways.

No one has asked either of them how the class is going lately. There haven't been any major challenges to create a concern on the part of leaders. And no one seems to notice they have come into the worship service late rather consistently. One day as they met together, Amy asked Fran, "Does any one really care if we teach, or do they care about what's going on in the lives of these children?" They determined that their commitment to the Lord and those kids keeps them going. But it does get discouraging.

Bill was the administrator of a local hospital and also a Sunday school teacher in this same church. When he was asked to compare his hospital's volunteer program with his ministry as a teacher of fifth and sixth graders, his response was: "If our volunteers were treated like our church treats Sunday school teachers, we wouldn't have any volunteers."

Why Appreciation Is So Important

+ + + + + + +

It's so easy for leadership to take volunteers for granted and show them little appreciation. Why should we take better care of our volunteers? Why should we express appreciation to them? Because we care about them. Everyone needs to be wanted and thanked. Our volunteers need to hear how meaningful and valuable their role is in the church's ministry.

Very few churches pay their teachers. But there is a sense in which they need to be paid—not with money, but with appreciation, thanks, and affirmation. These are the valuable rewards a volunteer needs and deserves. Payment with these dividends goes a long way in helping people feel satisfied and fulfilled in their ministry.

There are many ways to demonstrate our appreciation for ministry involvement. And if you are like most people in a leadership role, you are continually looking for new ways to encourage, demonstrate support, affirm, and say thanks. This chapter will highlight some proven ways to accomplish this objective. You are encouraged to try some of these ideas and use them as springboards to generate your own unique ideas.

Major Events

+ + + + + + +

As crucial as volunteers are in any church's ministry, such work needs to be recognized in a big way. Plan a major event that is meant to recognize the contributions of your volunteers at least once each year—a banquet, picnic, retreat, or special service to honor all involved in volunteer ministries, including assistants, substitutes, and those assigned special responsibilities. Make it a gala event and be sure to budget accordingly.

Brainstorm with your committee about these ideas and other themes to put together a great celebration of God at work in your Bible teaching ministry.

Major events do not need to be a banquet motif. Maybe you will want to have a special Sunday brunch. Perhaps a picnic at the park or other setting would work for you. A dessert setting with staff, elders, spouses is also a great opportunity. Many of the following theme ideas could easily fit into any location.

To make these events successful, draw on the skills and interests of as many people as possible. Allow people to exercise their creativity and develop an event that will be an expression of genuine appreciation and thanks from the entire congregation.

Love Boat—"Cruise on the Corinthian XIII"

Show your volunteers that not only do you need them and their abilities but that you truly love them in Christ. Build your entire evening around taking a cruise and have a Bon Voyage reception. Try some of the following ideas to make the event memorable.

- Have a drawing for seats at the captain's table.
- Make the dining room a festive place creating a cruise décor with nautical items.
- Include an ice sculpture. Use good china and silver. The menu should be gourmet.
- After the main course have a portion of the program.
- Prepare a dessert buffet with choice of fine desserts.
- Use guest musicians and speaker (perhaps the Apostle Paul speaking on 1 Corinthians 13).
- Awards and recognition should fit the theme.

Night of Stars—a take off on the Oscars

Treat your volunteers like stars. Plan an elegant evening that focuses on their work for the past year, including such features as:

- Valet parking
- Red carpet
- Gourmet meal
- Special music (harp, piano, string quartet)
- Speaker—message based on 1 Corinthians 12 or 2 Peter 5:2-4
- Fine awards, based on nominations from parents or other church members (Teacher of the Year, Best Supporting Teacher, Lifetime Achievement Award, and other special awards)

Chuck Wagon BBQ—informal western theme

The chuck wagon is a kitchen on wheels used to provide cowboys a hot, hearty meal after a tough day working the herd. Recognize your volunteers' hard work by providing a fun western-style meal.

- Encourage everyone to wear their favorite western garb (cowboy boots, hats, denim, etc.)
- BBQ menu, served from foil pans
- Country music
- Cowboy skits

An Evening in Paris—a sidewalk café setting with a backdrop representing Paris

Sometimes the day-to-day work in ministry can seem dreary and ordinary. Treat your volunteers to a special "vacation" by providing a backdrop of an elegant or exotic location.

- French menu (menu and program printed in French)
- Servers dressed in black and white
- Sidewalk musicians
- Show travelogue video of Paris
- Use dramatic presentation fitting to theme

Other themes to build on:

- Aloha—Hawaiian Holiday
- An Evening at the Movies
- Spring (or Fall) Carnival
- Bible Times Visit
- Spring in the Country
- An Olympic Award Ceremony
- Kids are Special
- Classroom Memories
- An Apple Delight
- Music for God's Glory

Minor Events and Other Ideas

✦ ✦ ✦ ✦ ✦ ✦ ✦

In addition to a major event, plan on offering frequent and on-going expressions of thanks and appreciation all through the year. Sometimes a year is a long time between expressions of gratitude and support. Make sure your volunteers know that they are valuable all day, every day, all year long.

Minor Events

Public recognition does not always have to be a big bash. Sometimes all it takes is a simple expression of thanks or some other "pat on the back."

• Hold a dedication or commissioning service for teachers each year. Make sure the whole church sees that classes are not simply staffed, but they are active ministry efforts by dedicated ministers.

• Invite volunteers to the leader's home for casual opportunities to build relationships by class or department.

• On a Saturday in December recruit other volunteers from adult and teen departments to baby-sit so your volunteer staff can go Christmas shopping.

Notes and Cards

There's something special about a tangible expression of thanks in a simple handwritten note or a card. Purchase cards specifically for individuals or buy a package of note cards that show your personal nature.

• A personal note thanking the teaching for involvement (from ministry leader, pastor, etc.)

• A personal note recognizing some action or achievement.

• A birthday card, Thanksgiving card, Valentine's Day card, etc.

• A shower of notes from students and/or parents—surprise the teacher on a selected Sunday.

• A note of thanks to the teacher's spouse or family letting them know how much you appreciate their willingness to allow this person to be involved in ministry.

• Make use of e-mail to send special notes or a greeting card for a birthday, anniversary, special thanks, or any other occasion.

• Personal notes from the pastor and other leaders are greatly appreciated.

Special Treats

Distribute a card with an appropriate treat. For example, on Super Bowl Sunday give a chocolate football attached to a card that says, "Thanks for doing a SUPER job in our children's ministry." Or, if an individual or a group has done something special for you, give them a package of Life-Savers brand candies with a note that reads, "You saved my life when...." (See *Treat 'Em Right* by Susan Cutshall, which contains 70 different creative suggestions for other thankful treats [Standard Publishing, 1999].)

Try some of these ideas for making your own special thank-you treats using clipart and special type. (Attach the treat in parentheses to your note.)

- Thanks for bringing so much JOY to our children. (Almond Joy brand candy bar).

- A spoonful of kisses to thank you. The SUCCESS of our ministry depends on U!! (a plastic spoon with two Hershey Kiss's brand candies wrapped in netting)

- You put the Sunshine in our ministry. (artificial sunflower or a package of sunflower seeds)

- Hats off to you! You are tops in our book. (a small hat from a party store or a craft supply store)

- Thanks a bunch! We're bananas for you! (a banana)

- You're my cup of tea. (a teabag)

- God's Greatest Treasure... (text on cover of a folded card; inside, a small mirror or a square of shiny aluminum foil and the words "Is you!")

- We're bubbling over with gratitude for your contributions to our ministry. (a small bottle of bubble bath or bubble solution with a wand)

- Your teaching is making a world of difference! (any world button or pin; a globe pencil sharpener)

- Thank you for your creative touch. (a small paint palette and paintbrush)

- A teacher plants the tiny (seeds) that bring forth the (flowers).

- Thanks for going to bat for our kids! (a small baseball bat from a party store)

- Hang in there! (clothespin)

- "Raisin" godly children can be fun! (small box of raisins)

- Like a magnet you are drawing children to God. (small magnet)

- Your teaching is worth more than all the money in the world to God. (play money)

- 2 HUGS...one for receiving and one for giving. (Hershey's Hug brand candies)

- A hug and a kiss because we appreciate you. (Hershey's Kiss and Hug brand candies)

- We are "sew" happy you are part of our team. (a small spool of thread)

- Thanks for keeping our ministry on track. (a small toy RR track piece)

- Thanks! We tip our hats to you. (a small hat from craft supply store)

- We're so glad you are taking care of our "babes" in Christ. (a small baby item such as toy rattle, bottle, or pacifier)

- Thank you for planting seeds of faith. (a package of seeds)

- You are God's treasure. (several toy gold coins or gold-foil-covered candy coins)

Prayer Support

Volunteers need to know that you and others are praying for them and their ministries. Establish a plan for providing prayer support. Use a variety of methods for encouraging your entire church to support your volunteer staff.

• Recruit a prayer partner for each teacher. Many people who are unable to work in the classroom do have a deep commitment to Bible teaching and would welcome the opportunity to partner with a teacher or a team of teachers to pray regularly and to stay in communication with the workers to be current with needs.

• Have a special place for a basket with slips of paper where all teachers may give and receive prayer requests.

• Recognize hurts, disappointments, and other needs. Be sure to communicate your concern with a phone call, note, or visit.

• Include prayer requests in your newsletters, and also include answers to prayer.

Communication With the Entire Church Family

Don't keep your volunteers a secret. Share their special abilities and ministry with the whole church. Use a variety of communication outlets to promote your volunteers.

• Publish articles in the church newsletter or bulletin about ministries and include names of volunteers. For example, you could write, "The fourth and fifth graders have been involved in an exciting unit on Paul's missionary journeys. Stop by their classroom (E22) to see the results of some effective Bible learning led by Stacey and Jack Holcomb and Jan Juarez." This takes very little time, minimal space, and not much effort. But teachers and learners will feel valued and appreciated.

• Spotlight the volunteer ministries during a worship service in a variety of ways, such as with a multi-media presentation that includes a video of classes in action, perhaps accompanied by an appropriate song from a recording or a live soloist. Use skits to showcase your volunteers. Interview a teacher or her students, asking questions about their teacher. Allow a teacher to give a testimony, highlighting some recent happenings. On a day when you are celebrating the teaching staff, make a display in the front of the worship center with a bright red apple for each volunteer.

• Prepare a bulletin board to show your appreciation for teachers in your children's ministry. Prepare text and tape the suggested candy or treat (or the empty packaging of them!) in the appropriate places. Adapt this example, as appropriate for your ministry. As space allows place pictures of the teaching staff around this rebus message:

Sweet Rewards!

Dear Children's Ministry STARS (Starburst brand candies),

It's a delight to have such a team of CRACKER JACK (Cracker Jack brand snacks) teachers in our classrooms. This season we have an EGG-ceptional (Reese's brand peanut butter egg or other egg shaped candy) group of people who are a JOY (Almond Joy brand candy) to serve with. They truly have a HEART (chocolate heart) for ministry and BEARY (gummy bears) glad to touch the lives of children for our Lord's glory. Just imagine what a ZOO (animal cookies) this place would become without their careful and prayerful ministry. Take time to HUG (Hershey's Hug brand candy) a teacher today, because they're always there in the CRUNCH (Nestle's Crunch brand candy), and they always go the EXTRA (Extra brand gum) mile.

With love and thanks for your part in our symphony of God's love,

Symphony Director (Symphony brand candy bar)

Make a Presentation of Gifts

Small gifts express appreciation in a tangible way. They do not need to be extravagant or expensive, but they need to express genuine thanks. Such gifts may include books, bookmarks, flowers, calendars, mugs, or magnets. They may be purchased or custom made. Often creative craft people in the church delight in making special gifts that can be personalized. Perhaps a group of people could come together to work on such a project.

Some ideas for special gifts include:

• A barbecue apron or T-shirt for each teacher, autographed by the students—a valued treasure when children decorate with messages, drawings, and names.

• Pictures of the class in action, attractively mounted and framed.

• A personalized Christmas ornament, handmade or purchased.

• Gift certificates from your local Christian store, ice cream shop, or video store. These can also be given as family gifts in appreciation for their sharing of the workers to the ministry.

• A plate of homemade cookies, small loaf of bread, hot chocolate mix, spiced tea mix, or other edible goodies.

• You can also let students know about their teacher's birthday and have them treat their teacher with a gift. Let the students know either by phone or by mail.

• A day off. An active list of substitute teachers can be a big help to relieve some of the pressures of teaching. The typical church will have very capable people who will enjoy being a substitute because they cannot commit to fulltime responsibilities. These people can be used so that a regular teacher can have a Sunday off without guilt pangs. Often, just knowing that there are substitutes available brings a feeling of relief and appreciation.

Other Ideas

Stay on the lookout for new and fresh ways to express thanks to those who give willingly of themselves for the ministry. It's an investment in retaining satisfied and effective workers for a long time.

- Post signs at the door to each classroom using class name and the names of each teacher.
- Give teachers a "Certificate of Recognition" that specifies the role they have had.
- Have volunteers wear attractive, durable name tags (as opposed to sticky, label-type ones). This communicates the church's value of the ministry. It also deals with safty concerns by providing for easy recognition of ministry staff members.
- Have a special bulletin board just for the teaching staff—a place to share important information and news for those involved in the teaching ministry.
- Provide a weeknight or weekday Bible study group just for those involved in the teaching ministry.
- Include money in your budget for saying "thank you." These volunteers serve behind the scenes and are responsible for a major portion of the church's ministry. They deserve recognition and appreciation. Funds for this purpose should not be considered discretionary to be easily pulled off the budget. Teachers and all those who work in the educational ministry give heavily of their time and energy and should be rewarded accordingly.

"And now, friends, we ask you to honor those leaders who work so hard for you, who have been given the responsibility of urging and guiding you along in your obedience. Overwhelm them with appreciation and love!" (1 Thessalonians 5:12, 13, "The Message").

Chapter Eight

Training Volunteers with Specialized Sessions

The final section of this book will provide suggestions and outlines for twelve teacher-enrichment sessions. Select those that meet the needs of your volunteers. Adapt or change as needed to fit your specific ministry. Each session will be based on the following outline.

- *Lesson Title*
- *Aims: Three or four statements completing the statement "Participants will have opportunity to...."*
- *Gather Materials: List of materials needed for the session.*
- *Prepare: Preparations to make before the session begins.*
- *As They Arrive: Beginning activity to introduce topic of the session.*
- *Share Information: A variety of ways to explore the topic.*
- *Plan to Use the Information: Specific ways to choose to apply or use the experiences and information from the session*
- *Group Prayer and Planning Time: Volunteer teams can pray together and perhaps have enough time to plan specifically for the next teaching session.*

2. Prepare.

3. Depend on the Lord.

B. God's promise is: "So is my word that goes out from my mouth: It will not return to me empty, but will accomplish what I desire and achieve the purpose for which I sent it" (Isaiah 55:11).

Plan to Use the Information

Ask participants to gather with their teaching team. Together, select three examples of Jesus' teaching that can be applied to specific students in their classes.

Group Prayer and Planning Time

Invite participants to share prayer needs. Include prayer for learners. Ask God to direct each team to use the methods of Jesus. Pray that skills will increase and that each teaching team will continue to serve together effectively.

If enough time has been scheduled for lesson planning, encourage participants to plan generally for the next teaching unit or specifically for the next teaching session.

TEACH LIKE JESUS TAUGHT

1. Jesus Taught with Urgency (Matthew 7:28, 29).

2. Jesus accepted his pupils as they were, and he led them to what they ought to be (John 8:3-11).

3. Jesus demonstrated that good teaching does not depend upon good facilities.

4. Jesus used methods that were suited to his students.

5. Jesus was the Divine Master Teacher.

God's promise is: "So is my word that goes out from my mouth: It will not return to me empty, but will accomplish what I desire and achieve the purpose for which I sent it" (Isaiah 55:11).

2. Unwrap the Gift of Teaching

+ + + + + + +

Aims

Participants will have opportunity to:

• Explore God-given gifts

• Identify gifts they can give to learners

• Select gifts they will give to specific learners

Gather Materials

Bibles

one medium-size gift box

eight small gift boxes

assorted gift boxes, as needed

wrapping paper (happy face/seasonal)

cards with Scripture verses on them

Prepare

Before the session make copies of two response sheets for each participant. Make transparencies of the response sheets if you wish to use them. Type the reference and entire Scripture verses on cards: Proverbs 15:2; Daniel 12:3; Luke 6:40; Romans 12:6-8; 1 Corinthians 11:1; 1 Corinthians 12:4-7; James 3:1; 1 Peter 4:10, 11. Place them in eight small gift boxes, wrap them, and number them 1 to 8.

Read through Romans 12:4-8. Plan for a way for participants to read this passage responsively.

Place a Bible in the medium-size gift box and wrap it. Gather items indicated for the second part of the session (gifts to be given to learners). They may be objects or pictures that represent the gift. Wrap them and number from 1 to 14.

As They Arrive

Direct participants to look at the wrapped packages. Ask them to guess the contents of the medium-size gift. Record responses on a whiteboard or chalkboard. Open the box to find the Bible. If possible have Bibles available for each person.

Share Information

Explain that the purpose of this session is to explore Scriptures to discover gifts and lessons about teaching from the Bible. Tell the group that during the first part of the session, they will open eight boxes, read the Scriptures inside, and discover the message. Open the eight small boxes, read the Scriptures, and discuss them.

1. Proverbs 15:2: Bring joy to learning—active, meaningful, fun, age-appropriate.
2. Daniel 12:3: Describing end times—we are expected to use gifts well, pleasing God.
3. Luke 6:40: Opportunity for growth—model a Christ-like life.
4. Romans 12:6-8: We must use our gifts; have opportunity to encourage, show mercy, etc.
5. 1 Corinthians 11:1: Follow Christ's example so that learners can follow our example.
6. 1 Corinthians 12:4-7: All gifts work together—contribute to the body.
7. James 3:1: Teachers must realize responsibility and work hard—be diligent.
8. 1 Peter 4:10, 11: Use gifts to serve others; faithfully administering God's grace; words of God; serve with strength; praise God through Jesus Christ; give God the glory.

Complete the first section of the session by reading 1 Corinthians 12:4-7 responsively.

During the second part of this session we will discover gifts we can give to our learners. Open each of the boxes numbered 1 to 14, one at a time, in order. (The following list will begin with the object, followed by the gift.)

1. Bible—Bible-centered and life-application teaching
2. Praying Hands—prayer (specific and individual)
3. Curriculum (teachers' book)—well-prepared lessons
4. Picture of Classrooms—comfortable classroom
5. Picture of Children (perhaps a collage)—understanding of age/learning process
6. Picture of Excited Child/Teen in Action—exciting learning experiences
7. Creativity—creatively lettered poster indicating creativity
8. Ear (plastic ears usually available in October)—gift of listening
9. Happy Face Figure—encouragement
10. Card or Note Paper—caring contacts
11. Clock—gift of time
12. Heart Shaped Cookies/Candy/Stickers—unconditional love/acceptance
13. Romans 15:4 lettered on card in small box—gift of hope
14. 1 Corinthians 13:4-7 lettered on card in small box—gifts of patience, kindness, humility, courtesy, fresh start, truth, protection, trust, perseverance

3. Make Curriculum Work for You

+ + + + + + +

Aims

Participants will have opportunity to:

- Discover elements of curriculum.
- Consider relationship of curriculum to students needs.
- Become aware of ways to adapt curriculum.
- Invest time to plan/prepare a teaching session.

Gather Materials

Bibles

Curriculum for each class

Paper/pens for lesson planning

Bag or box and note cards

Thirteen 14-by-l6-inch clasp envelopes for each teacher (optional)

Felt pens to label envelopes (optional)

Prepare

Before the session, make copies of the outline for a note-taking handout. Provide paper and pens for lesson planning. Provide an attractive bag or box. Place note cards by it with a sign that reads "Write questions about your curriculum and place them in the bag." If you choose to use envelopes to organize curriculum, label a set of fourteen. Envelopes 1 through 13 should be labeled: Lesson 1, Lesson 2, etc. Label the fourteenth envelope "Additional materials."

As They Arrive

Ask participants to pick up a stack of thirteen envelopes. They need to label them as the example. Explain that the envelopes are to be used to organize all of the parts and pieces of the curriculum. Elements will vary according to the age/grade level. There should be time to label the envelopes. Participants will need to sort and organize later.

Share Information

1. Introduction—Curriculum is only a guide. It provides a systematic approach to teaching, with objectives and methods of reaching those objectives. Curriculum writers can only write for a "typical" student of a specific age level. The course cannot be exactly right for every specific class. Adapt curriculum to the particular needs and characteristics of your students. Consider your facilities and your own teaching style.

2. Be familiar with the characteristics of your students. Know general age-level characteristics. Know your students individually. Invest time in becoming acquainted. Answer the following questions about each one.
    A. Do they have difficulty reading?
    B. How much Bible do they know?
    C. What kinds of activities do they enjoy? (drama, art, writing, verbal, games, etc.)
    D. What are their learning styles? (auditory, visual, tactile, kinesthetic)
    E. What are special learning needs?
    F. What are their attention spans?
    G. What are behavior challenges that need to be considered? Add others that are important to you.

3. Consider other characteristics of your students and adjust lesson materials accordingly. Answer the following questions about each one.
    A. Are they quiet?
    B. Are they very active?
    C. What is their home situation?
    D. Be alert to cultural backgrounds, income levels, etc.

4. Be aware of the facilities you have to work with. The curriculum may assume certain things that you do not have or may not suggest use of things you do have. Plan ahead for equipment you may need or want to use. Request supplies that are not usually available in your classroom or resource room. Think about a variety of ways to arrange furniture in the classroom. How can you create more usable space?

5. Keep in mind your own skills and teaching style. Know your strengths and weaknesses. Use strengths. Work to strengthen weaknesses. Adapt printed materials to fit your skills. Know your gifts. Ask God to use you in a way that will honor him.

6. Remember that curriculum is a tool. The world is your resource library. Familiarize yourself with your church's resources. Request items that need to be added.

7. Conclusion
    A. No two classes are alike.
    B. No two students are alike.
    C. No two teachers are alike.
    D. Tailor your teaching to your skills and to the unique and special students God has entrusted to you!

Plan to use the information

Ask participants to gather in teaching team groups. If there are some participants who are not directly connected to a team, ask them to select a team that ministers with an age level in which they have interest.

1. Ask participants to locate a lesson they will teach in the near future. Ask them to do the following.
    - Read aims and objectives.
    - Identify activities.
    - Make note of learners that would benefit from each of the activities.
    - Plan to use the activities that will speak the needs and interests of the greatest number of learners.
    - Review the suggested time schedule. Make necessary adaptations that will work with your time schedule.
    - Consider ways the teaching style affects the lesson plan.
    - Check to be sure a variety of learning styles are utilized.
2. If time permits, teams can work on organizing curriculum into the thirteen envelopes. Some may choose to use another method of organization. Encourage volunteers to do what will work for them. However, be clear that some method of organization will save preparation time each week and will also help to make the transition to a substitute teacher easier.

Group Prayer

Be sure to reserve some time for prayer.

1. Introduction

2. Be familiar with the characteristics of your students.

3. Consider other characteristics of your students and adjust lesson materials accordingly.

4. Be aware of your facilities.

5. Keep in mind your own skills and teaching style.

6. Remember that curriculum is a tool.

7. Conclusion

strong relationships. "Stick to it!" Write the names of students with whom you desire to build a strong relationship on the notes. Place it in a prominent place as a reminder to pray and work to build a relationship.

About the Process

1. Distribute crayons. Discuss room environment. (Add color to your classroom.) Make your classroom a colorful place. If possible, look at some classrooms and evaluate possible changes at the close of the session.

2. Distribute plastic spoons. Teach with bite-size portions. Discuss age appropriate and focused learning.

3. Distribute sponge pieces. Learners "soak up" good learning experiences. Ask small groups to brainstorm responses to the question, "What are good learning experiences for your group?"

4. Distribute balloons. Fill your learners' balloons. Learning experiences at church should "fill" the learners so that they are soaring like a helium balloon that has been released. Discuss ways to fill learners as balloons.

Plan to Use the Information

Read and comment on 1 Corinthians 13:4-7. Ask participants to select one item from their "survival kit" and plan for a specific way to use it soon.

Group Prayer and Planning Time

Share and pray with a partner or in a group of three. If time permits, invest time in lesson evaluation and planning.

5. Design Lessons to Meet Students' Needs

+ + + + + + +

Aims

Participants will have opportunity to:

- Discover ways to know students.
- Explore aspects of lesson planning and preparation.
- Plan a strategy to know learners well.
- Select one way to increase effectiveness of lesson planning/preparation.

Gather Materials

Three direction cards

copies of handout page 118

"Remember" cards

poster board/felt pens

paper and pens

blank transparencies/pens

overhead projector

Bible, devotional guide

list of students

pictures of students (optional)

Prepare

Before the session make copies of the "Remember" statements. Make it on card stock, if possible. Prepare copies of the handout on page 118 for taking notes. Arrange chairs in three groups. Label each group 1, 2, or 3. Place supplies suggested for each group in that work area. Prepare three direction cards. Letter the following directions on them:

1. Brainstorm specific ways to know your learners. Plan for a way to share your discussion with the total group. You may present a role-play or interview. You may develop an information sheet to complete for each learner. Sit in the area marked "1."

2. Brainstorm ways to prepare yourself to teach. Focus on your spiritual growth rather than on a specific lesson. Think about using the Bible, devotional guide, and list of students. Plan for a way to share your discussion with the total group. You may present

a role-play or use blank transparencies and pens to project your responses. Sit in the area marked "2."

3. Brainstorm ways to plan and prepare a lesson. Try to determine a step to be completed on each of six days. Plan for a way to share your six steps with the total group. You may make a poster listing the six steps or use a blank transparency and transparency pens. Sit in the area marked "3."

As They Arrive

Ask participants to sit in one of the three areas. Ask them to sit with people they do not serve with, if possible. For the first few minutes, encourage them to share the best thing that happened during their last teaching session.

Share Information

Be sure participants have the materials they need and they understand the directions. You may say something like this to encourage participation and clarify directions: "During this session we will be considering three aspects of the teaching ministry. Each group has been assigned one of these areas (Know your students; Prepare yourself, Plan your lesson). You will work together for about 15 minutes. Then each group will share information. During the sharing we may provide some additional information."

Give a 5-minute warning at the end of 10 minutes, and after 15 minutes, let the three groups share. Following is some information you may wish to add, if the groups do not include it. Distribute note-taking handouts just before the groups share.

1. Know your students.
    A. Be a good listener.
    B. Spend time with them.
    C. Know their interests. (Develop a notebook with a page for each student. Use it to record pertinent information. Add pages as needed.)
    D. Follow their activities.
    E. Know their families.
2. Prepare yourself.
    A. Study the lesson for personal growth.
    B. Pray for divine guidance and personal instruction.
    C. Pray daily for your students by name.

D. Begin each day of the week with a devotional time by reading the Scripture text for the following Sunday's lesson.

3. Plan your lesson.

    A. Identify your students' needs.

    B. Determine your lesson aims/goals. (Consider the identified needs.)

    C. Gather your teaching materials.

    D. Choose your teaching method.

    E. Plan your lesson presentation.

    F. Evaluate your results.

        1. What two things went well?

        2. What one thing needed improvement?

Remember

Needs determine goals.

Goals suggest materials.

Materials dictate methods.

Methods require presentation.

Presentation necessitates evaluation.

Evaluation (honest) results in improvement.

It all requires commitment and time!

Remember

Needs determine goals.

Goals suggest materials.

Materials dictate methods.

Methods require presentation.

Presentation necessitates evaluation.

Evaluation (honest) results in improvement.

It all requires commitment and time!

- Kinesthetic learner: needs to be moving during the learning process in ways such as action songs, drama, and games.

2. Label one each of four poster boards with the learning styles.

As They Arrive

If participants are not well acquainted, ask them to prepare and wear name tags. Ask participants to examine the two oranges and write down how they are similar and how they are different. During the follow-up discussion, ask how many picked up the oranges to examine them. How many only looked at them? How many discussed the differences with others?

Share Information

Begin by saying, "Children, like oranges, are similar and different." Ask participants to share characteristics of their students. Identify similarities and differences. Respond to the questions "What characteristics are frequently related to age/grade levels?" and "What characteristics are related to individuals rather than to age groups?"

Divide participants into four equal groups. Give each group one of the four pieces of poster board on which you have lettered one of the four learning styles. They will also need a felt pen.

Discuss the information on the transparency. Place a blank piece of paper under the transparency, covering the information about auditory, tactile, and kinesthetic learners while you are discussing visual learners. Slide the paper down, one learning style at a time until information about all four has been discussed. Encourage participants to give additional examples of appropriate activities as each learning style is discussed.

Summarize the discussion with these or similar statements. Maximum learning is always the result of maximum involvement of the learners. Activities that utilize a variety of learning styles in each session causes the greatest amount of involvement. The presupposition is that the activity in which the students are involved is meaningful. It must be related to the Scripture being taught and/or application of the Scripture.

Distribute enough Bibles so that each group has several. Ask participants to read Luke 5:1-11. After reading the passage, ask participants to list activities described in the passage using the learning style listed on each groups' poster board.

Discuss activities as time permits. If time and interest allow, ask participants to add activities of their learning style from other events of Jesus' teaching.

Plan to Use the Information

Direct participants to look at the lesson in their teachers' book for next week's teaching session. Encourage them to select activities that use a variety of learning styles. Be sure that meaningful involvement is part of each activity.

Group Prayer and Planning Time

Encourage participants to work on lesson planning for the remainder of the session. Pray, asking God to help you provide activities that will enable learners to know and apply God's Word.

Visual Learners

+ + + + + + +

Respond to visual stimuli. They need visual dues, lists, charts, and maps, objects, directions, etc. to help them under stand and remember. Include color, pictures, bulletin board displays and other resources.

Auditory Learners

+ + + + + + +

Respond best to sound. Can follow verbal directions. Enjoy learning from cassettes and music. Classroom sounds are learning sounds, not distracting noises.

Tactile Learners

+ + + + + + +

Enjoy touching and feeling as they learn. Enjoy using clay, reaching into containers, identifying objects, and telling stories. Tracing/drawing in sand/cornmeal can enhance learning.

Kinesthetic Learners

+ + + + + + +

Learning takes place when the whole child is involved in the activity. Enjoy active games, hopscotch, musical chairs- large muscle and drama activities

7. Making Bible Memory Come Alive

+ + + + + + +

Aims

Participants will have opportunity to:

- Discover exciting, fun ways to memorize Scripture.
- Experience a variety of Bible memory activities.
- Select at least three new ways to use in class to encourage students to memorize Scripture.
- Develop a game to use in the classroom. (optional)

Gather Materials

Bibles

copies of handout, page 126

three- or four-word scramble games

collection of Bible games from resource room or classrooms (Ask teachers to bring games they use in their classes.)

materials needed to make games (optional)

Prepare

1. Remind teachers to bring Bible memory games and curriculum.
2. Arrange room with tables for participants to work around.
3. Make copies of the handout on page 126.
4. Make three or four "Word Scramble" games. Letter the words of Psalm 119:11 on three or four different colors of card stock. Cut it apart so there are approximately twelve pieces. Place one color at each of three or four tables in the room. As participants arrive, encourage them to work at one of the tables to put the verse together. Place a bookmark in a Bible for each of the areas. When the activity is completed, check for accuracy.
5. Gather/make several of the games listed and plan for participants to experience the games. They will be more likely to use games in their classrooms when they have experienced them.

As They Arrive

Ask participants to move to an area of the room that has one of the scrambled word games. Have them put the verse together in order. Use the Bible to check accuracy. This verse states very clearly that memorization of Scripture is a very important aspect of preparing to live a life that is pleasing to God. Encourage volunteers who have not memorized this verse to make a commitment to memorize it this week. By the way, it is important for adults to memorize the Scripture they are asking learners to memorize!

Share Information

If teachers of a wide age range are involved in this session, be sure to include activities that are suitable for all of those ages. Begin this part of the session by playing several games together. Then move to games that involve a small number of people. Ask for six to eight volunteers to participate.

• Popcorn Verse—Select a verse that will be familiar to the participants (perhaps John 3:16 or Psalm 119:11). Divide the group in half (approximately half is good enough). Begin the game with everyone seated. Point to one half of group. They must pop up and begin to say the verse. Stop pointing to the first group and point to the second half. The first group sits down quickly as the second group pops up. This game can be more or less challenging depending on the speed with which the leader changes sides and the length of verse used.

• Match a Verse—Write several verses that your students have used in the last quarter on card stock. Ask students to write several "Real Life" situations on separate cards. Then pass them all out, read them aloud, and ask students to match the situations with each verse.

• Wheel of Fortune Game—Use an overhead projector and transparency, poster board, white board, or chalk board. Plot out your memory verse by drawing a line for each letter and leaving spaces between each word. Write the alphabet along the side and then divide the students into two groups. Play "Wheel of Fortune," with each side guessing letters and filling them in when a correct letter is guessed. Vowels are the last to be used.

• Circle the Ball Match—Write the words of the memory verse on separate pieces of construction paper. Attach yarn to the paper so the participants can put them around their neck. Form a circle. With a ball, begin at the first word of the memory verse, and as each person says their word, they must throw the ball to the person with the next word in the verse. Practice this a few times, then mix everyone up in the circle and exchange words. Do it again. Place papers upside down on the floor. Say the verse.

• Overhead Projector Game—Divide the memory verse into sections and let each group draw a picture, depicting their part of the verse on a blank transparency. Use transparency pens. Let each group learn their part of the verse. Then put the pictures in order and as you show each one, the appropriate group stands up and says their part of the verse. Change groups and repeat.

• Paper Plate Game—Give each student a paper plate and felt pens. Let them decorate their plate according to the theme of the verse and attach a paint stick or craft stick to the back, using duct or masking tape. Divide the group into sets of two and give each group a balloon. When they have their balloon inflated, they should bat the balloon back and forth as they say the words of the memory verse.

• Stick To It—Ask students to letter words of the memory verse on thirty self-stick notes, one word per tab. Stick the tabs on a door or wall with words mixed up. Other students sequence the words correctly, mix them up, and then still others sequence them correctly.

• Balloon Pop—Letter references of verses that have been memorized on small slips of paper. Roll them up and insert them in empty balloons. Blow up and tie the balloons. Students take turns popping a balloon and then saying the verse that matches the reference in the balloon. Use Bibles to check accuracy.

• Tape It!—Auditory learners will enjoy recording memory verses on a blank cassette tape. Work in teams to read, record, listen, and check.

Plan to Use the Information

These ten games provide a small beginning. Encourage volunteers to share additional games. Experience as many as possible. Near the end of the session, ask teachers to select three to five games they would like to plan to use in their classrooms. Provide materials that may be needed.

Group Prayer and Planning Time

Pray together, asking God to convict you to make Bible memory one of the most exciting aspects of your learning sessions. Use the remainder of the time to explore games, make games, experience games, or plan for the next teaching session.

Respond to the following questions.

1. What are some exciting ways to encourage Bible memory?

2. How can awareness of learning styles help to select games?

List three games you would like to use in your classroom.

1.

2.

3.

Plan for specific Bible memory activities that will be especially appropriate to teach and reinforce Bible memory in your next several lessons.

8. Involvement Learning

+ + + + + +

Aims

Participants will have opportunity to

- Recall and share a recent learning experience.
- Review information about four learning styles.
- Explore a teaching experience of Jesus.
- Plan specific ways to increase students' involvement in class.

Gather Materials

Bibles

copies of teaming style information on card stock

copies of appropriate learning activities for various ages

copies of handout, page 129

materials for at least one activity from curriculum of each age level

pictures or drawings of the following items: car, bicycle, swimming pool, pie, sewing
   machine, computer, any other items that require learning a skill

writing paper and pens

Prepare

Make copies of learning style information on card stock. The reproducible sheet will make two copies at a time. Also, make copies of the learning activities lists. They are on the reproducible page with the learning style information and will provide two copies at a time. Copy and cut into fourths. Also make copies of the handout.

Contact at least one teacher from each age/grade level involved in the session. Ask each of them to prepare to lead one learning activity from their teachers' books. This will accomplish two things. The teachers involved will prepare and practice an activity to use with their students, and all participants will be able to explore a greater number of activities.

Provide enough pictures or drawings so that no more than six to eight participants will be working with each one. If your group is large, duplicate pictures. Display pictures around the room on walls or tables. Place paper and pens near each picture.

As They Arrive

Ask participants to gather by a picture that shows something they can remember learning. They need to discuss how they learned to complete the tasks suggested by the picture. Agree on a sequence of steps that were taken to learn the skill. Ask three or four people to share the list of steps.

Share Information

Distribute cards with learning styles information. Not only did our earlier discussion point out the importance of involvement, but recognition that our learners come to us with a variety of learning styles serves to point out the importance of a variety of kinds of involvement in every learning experience.

Discuss information provided for each of the four learning styles. Encourage participants to share activities they have used in each of the learning styles.

Distribute note-taking handout. Instruct participants to read John 9:1-12. Each group may decide if they prefer to read silently or aloud.

On the handout, list ways Jesus involved the learners during the healing of the blind man (answered questions; mini-lecture; sense of touch; man went and washed). Invite participants to share a few other examples of involvement when Jesus taught.

Use the greatest amount of time for teachers to share activities from their curriculum. Encourage them to share adaptations they needed to make. At the end of the sharing of activities, distribute cards with lists of age-appropriate activities.

Plan to Use the Information

Ask participants to sit with others on their teaching team. Select and list activities that are age appropriate from each of the four learning styles to use in teaching their students. Use note-taking handout and cards for help.

Group Prayer and Planning Time

Ask God to help you determine which learning styles are most comfortable for individual learners in class. Pray that he will put a desire within each volunteer to be willing to stretch and experience new and different activities that will enhance the learning experiences of all students.

Use the remainder of the session to plan for specific lessons. Focus on involving learners in meaningful learning experiences.

Learning Styles

1. Which learning style is most comfortable for you?

2. How many learning styles will you plan to utilize in the future?

3. List names of learners under the appropriate learning style.

Visual   Auditory

Tactile   Kinesthetic

4. List involvement activities used in John 9:1-12

5. I will increase students' involvement in class by......

Learning Activities

Preschool: art, nature, music, family living, blocks, books, puzzles, games

Elementary: art, music, drama, creative writing, and verbal activities

Youth and Adult: art, music, drama, writing, and discussion

9. Relationships that Enhance Learning

+ + + + + + +

Aims

Participants will have opportunity to

- Experience three relationship building activities.
- Examine six relationship building skills.
- Commit to build relationships with peers, students, and their families.

Gather Materials

Bibles

6 to 8 each of eight different brands of miniature candy bars

decorative bag (container for candy bars)

6-by-9-inch writing paper and pens or pencils

twelve 9-by-12-inch signs, each with the name of a month lettered on it

copies of handout, page 133

Prepare

Put candy bars in bag. Place it by the entrance to the room with a direction card that asks participants to choose a favorite kind. Find two other people with the same kind of candy bar and tell the best thing that happened during the day before the session.

Letter the names of the months on signs and display on walls around the room. Leave space for a small group to gather around each one.

Copy handouts.

As They Arrive

Ask participants to choose a candy bar; locate two others with the same kind and follow directions to tell about the best thing that happened during the day.

Next distribute 6-by-9-inch paper and pens and ask the groups of three to list as many parts of the body as they can that are spelled with three letters. After about five to seven minutes, share lists.

Share Information

Form new groups by asking participants to stand by the sign that has the name of the month of his/her birthday. Share a birthday memory, using three or four sentences.

Discuss these three group activities. Selecting a candy bar was a nonthreatening, fun activity. Sharing a good thing is not difficult. Brainstorming to list three letter words is a non-threatening activity—completely impersonal and even a bit of fun. Now moving to the birthday sharing. This was still relatively nonthreatening, and yet, became more personal. The conclusion we can draw from these activities is that relationships are not built quickly. They require time and patience and begin with what may appear to be superficial sharing.

Distribute outline handouts. Ask participants to sit with their ministry team members. Guide discussion by giving some input and then encourage participants to further discuss the topic and make pertinent notes. We will examine six relationship building skills. The most effective learning occurs when strong positive relationships exist among the learners and volunteers who are part of the learning experience. We will focus on building relationships with our learners, but the same principles apply to relationships with family, friends, and co-workers.

Relationship Building Skills

1. Develop a proper attitude (a servant of God and people).

   Matthew 20:26

   Philippians 2:5-7

2. Develop a proper understanding.

   • Understand human nature (personality types, behavior patterns and characteristics)

   • Understand human need.

   • need to be loved

   • need to be needed

   • need to belong

   • need to be understood

   • need to be heard

   • need to be valued

   • need to be affirmed

   • need to be supported and encouraged

   • need to feel important

3. Develop communication skills.

   • Listen so people will talk—focused, attentive

- Talk so people will listen
- Eye and body movement—non-verbal communication is powerful.
- Deepen interest level
- must be genuine and sincere
- must be honest
- Communication must be
- honest (even if tough)
- open (two-way)
- continuous
- personal

4. Love people genuinely.

5. Know people personally.
   - Listen well.
   - Sacrifice time.
   - Know interests.
   - Follow activities.
   - Understand family situation.
   - Recognize strengths.
   - Recognize needs

6. Commit to them (John 10:11).
   - Commit long term.
   - Make people (students) your focus.

Plan to Use the Information

Ask participants to talk with one person next to them. Identify a teacher who made a difference in your life. Tell one person what you remember about that teacher. (After five minutes, suggest that most memories involve relationships.)

Now, identify specific ways you will plan to build relationships with specific students. Jot down the name of the student and the action somewhere on your outline.

Group Prayer and Planning Time

Encourage participants to pray about the commitments they have made to relationship building. Invest the remainder of the time in lesson planning. Focus on how relationship building can become an enhancement to the learning experience.

Relationship Building Skills

1. Develop a proper attitude.

2. Develop a proper understanding.

3. Develop communication skills.

4. Love people genuinely.

5. Know people personally.

6. Commit to them.

10. Top Ten Tips for Effective Classroom Discipline

+ + + + + + +

Aims

Participants will have opportunity to

• Examine selected Scriptures related to discipline.

• List top ten tips for effective discipline.

• Discover specific actions related to each of the tips.

• Plan a strategy for behavior management in their classrooms.

Gather Materials

copies of handout, page 137

Bibles

jar with marbles

popcorn or trail mix

simple dot-to-dot transparency, transparency pen

overhead projector

beanbag or sponge ball

poster board and felt pens or static cling sheets and whiteboard markers

Prepare

Display poster board or static cling sheets on the wall around the room. Use four to six sheets, depending on the size of your group. Place pens near the poster board or static cling sheets.

Make copies of handout. Place other materials on a table that will provide easy access.

Arrange room so that participants are sitting in groups of six to eight people. Chairs may be around tables or in half circles.

As They Arrive

Ask participants to write their most challenging behaviors on the poster board or static cling sheets. During the discussion of the top ten tips, be alert to identifying which tip will be effective with the listed behaviors. Enlist participants' help in checking the lists.

Share Information

Ask someone to read Matthew 18:1-5. Discuss Jesus' attitude toward children. Read Hebrews 12:11. Discipline is part of the process of discipling—making disciples. Our ministry with children and teens, and even with adults, is all about discipling them. Providing appropriate discipline principles as we interact with them will in fact draw them to God's love.

Say, "As we list ten tips, we will brainstorm and add specific things to do that will accomplish the goal of that particular tip."

10. Give appropriate, logical consequences for disruptive behavior.
    - Separate students as needed.
    - Remove them from one activity to another when they display inappropriate behavior.
    - Prevent disruptive behavior by providing for wiggles. Do some exercise together (30 seconds of silly exercise).
9. Help learners understand why specific behavior is not acceptable.
    - Refer to rules.
    - Ask "What happened?"—not "Why?"

Ask a small group to role play a conversation with a teacher and child. Identify an unacceptable behavior. Play out an alternative conversation that will help child understand why behavior is not acceptable.

8. Practice consistency in behavior expectations.
    - Maintain excitement with the unexpected—pop a balloon, flash a light.
    - Toss a beanbag or sponge ball when asking a question. Demonstrate.
7. Use age-appropriate behavior expectations.
    - Be aware of attention span.
    - Consider skills and interests.
6. Include all learning styles in the lesson plan.
5. Affirm positive behavior.
    - Complete dot-to-dot transparency. Provide treat.
    - Grab bag and "good" notes.
    - Bookmarks/buttons, etc.
4. Respect and accept each learner.
    - Use a timer to give warning before transition.
    - Make eye contact.
    - Be a focused listener.

- Give a fresh start.
  - Forgive and forget.
3. Build relationships.
  - Use names when speaking to each learner.
  - Invest time in knowing learners.
  - See learners in settings other than the classroom.
2. Plan and prepare prayerfully and carefully.
  - Be on time—at least 15 minutes early.
  - Begin when the first child arrives.
1. Pray.
  - Forgive and forget.
  - Pray regularly, specifically, and sincerely.
  - Refuse to label children. Help them build a positive reputation rather than a negative one.

Plan to Use the Information

Match challenging behaviors with one or more tips. Write a plan to meet behavior challenges in classrooms that use the tips. Include specific actions.

Discipline with love. Read 1 Corinthians 13:4-8 in unison. Discuss implications for behavior challenges.

1 Corinthians 13:4-8—"Love is patient, love is kind. It does not envy, it does not boast, it is not proud. It is not rude, it is not self-seeking, it is not easily angered, it keeps no record of wrongs. Love does not delight in evil but rejoices with the truth. It always protects, always trusts, always hopes, always perseveres. Love never fails."

Group Prayer and Planning Time

Pray together, earnestly seeking insight, wisdom, and guidance from God in relationship to responding to unacceptable behavior choices. Use the rest of the time to work on lesson planning. Be aware of the effect planning and preparation has on behavior.

TOP TEN TIPS FOR EFFECTIVE CLASSROOM DISCIPLINE

10. Give appropriate, logical consequences for disruptive behavior.

9. Help learners understand why specific behavior is not acceptable.

8. Practice consistency in behavior expectations.

7. Use age-appropriate behavior expectations.

6. Include all learning styles in the lesson plan.

5. Affirm positive behavior.

4. Respect and accept each learner.

3. Build relationships.

2. Plan and prepare prayerfully and carefully.

1. Pray.

11. Celebrate the Joy of Encouragement

+ + + + + + +

Aims

Participants will have opportunity to

- define encouragement.
- establish a biblical foundation for encouragement.
- recognize the relationship of encouragement to an effective education ministry.
- plan for additional ways to use the gift of encouragement

Gather Materials

Bibles

copies of handout, page 141

blank transparencies and transparency pens or 3 to 4 sheets of poster board and felt pens

overhead projector, if you are using transparencies

index cards with Scripture references

notepaper, pens, and stamps

several copies of church directory

balloons and items with happy faces

light refreshments

Prepare

Make copies of the handouts. Decorate the room with balloons and happy face items. Place refreshments in a convenient area. Place transparencies and pens on tables in three or four different areas of the room. Or, hang poster board on the walls in three or four different areas with felt pens nearby. On each transparency or poster board letter the unfinished sentence, "Encouragement is...." Letter the following references, one each on index cards: Romans 15:4; Romans 15:5; 2 Thessalonians 2:16, 17; 1 Thessalonians 5:11; Hebrews 3:13; Hebrews 10:25.

As They Arrive

Greet each participant individually. Make an encouraging comment to each one. If the group will be large, enlist other leaders to help you with this greeting so that no one will be left out. Invite participants to go to transparencies or a sheet of poster board. Write or draw to complete the sentence. Each participant may make more than one response as time allows.

Summarize this activity by reading and briefly discussing the responses. Volunteers may read from the poster board, or transparencies may be projected and read by the total group.

Share Information

Divide participants into three groups of six to eight people. If you need more than three groups, prepare enough duplicate cards with Scripture references for additional groups. Distribute two cards and Bibles to each group. Allow five to seven minutes for them to read and discuss the Scriptures. They may write notes on the cards and prepare to share something about what the Scripture teaches about encouragement. Talk about what the Scripture teaches about encouragement. Talk about each of the six verses one time.

Comment that Scripture certainly teaches that we need to be encouragers. Paul was an encourager. He was encouraged by Barnabas. Jesus was an encourager. He was encouraged. We receive encouragement through Scriptures. God gives encouragement and endurance for our task. Leaders need to encourage and be encouraged. Volunteers need to be encouragers and be encouraged. Students and families need to encourage and be encouraged. Certainly there is no more appropriate ministry than the teaching ministry to include encouragement as a significant part of the ministry. Encouragement is biblical.

Encouragement is more than a pat on the back. It is more than a compliment. Encouragement spurs someone on. It involves listening, caring, praying, and supporting. Encouragement is motivated by loving and caring. Encouragement is putting courage into some. What an awesome privilege!

Encouragement is stimulating hope. It helps in times of struggle and failure. Encouragement is sharing love, friendship, and wisdom.

Those who are part of the Christian education ministry encourage students, families, leaders, and other volunteers.

- Give personal responses.
- Build relationships.
- Pray for each other.
- Support.
- Help to build skills.
- Provide and share resources.

- Invest time.
- Ways to encourage:
1. Accept each other.
2. Give specific praise and affirmation.
3. Identify progress.
4. Work together. Teamwork is important.

You need encouragement, too. How can you "put courage into yourselves?"

- Spend time with God.
- Spend time with family.
- Spend time with friends.
- Spend time alone.
- Develop healthful habits and hobbies.
- Include adequate rest and refreshment in your schedule

Time seems to be a key ingredient in the ministry of encouragement. Involve others in the church family who have the gift of encouragement. It is important to include as many as possible in this important task of encouraging each other.

Invest time in each other. Plan for team building, networking, and building relationships (see chapter 4). Most importantly, invest time in prayer. Our relationship with God is the best source of encouragement and will enable us to be encouragers, too.

Plan to Use Information

Distribute note paper and stamps. Ask each participant to select a student or team member to encourage with a note. Invest eight to ten minutes if writing notes. If addresses are not known or available, ask participants to stamp notes and then add the address later. As notes are completed, participants may wish to enjoy refreshments.

Group Prayer and Planning Time

Invest the remainder of the time in praying and lesson planning. Focus on encouragement while praying and planning.

CELEBRATE THE JOY OF ENCOURAGEMENT

1. What does Scripture say about encouragement?

2. Encouragement is....

3. What will you do to encourage others?

4. How can you be encouraged?

5. List specific things you will do to encourage students and others.

12. The "One Anothers" of Ministry

✝ ✝ ✝ ✝ ✝ ✝ ✝

Aims

Participants will have opportunity to

- examine nine "one anothers" in Scripture.
- select at least three "one anothers" to put into practice with students and teaching teams.
- commit to accomplishing the selected "one anothers."

Gather Materials

Bibles

nine cards with scripture references

copies of handout, page 144

heart-shaped room decorations

heart-shaped refreshments (cookies, finger sandwiches, gelatin wigglers, etc.)

heart-shaped name tags

felt pens

Prepare

1. Make copies of handouts.
2. Collect heart-shaped decorations; arrange in room. (think about enlisting a committee to decorate)
3. Prepare or enlist a volunteer group to prepare refreshments.
4. Cut out name tags.
5. Letter the following Scripture references on nine cards. Make duplicate cards if you will have more than three groups of six to eight.
   - John 13:34, 35—Love one another.
   - Romans 15:7—Accept one another.
   - Galatians 5:13—Serve one another.
   - Galatians 6:2—Bear one anothers' burdens.
   - Ephesians 4:2—Be patient with one another.
   - Ephesians 4:32—Be kind and forgive one another.
   - Colossians 3:16—Teach one another.

- 1 Thessalonians 5:11, 14—Encourage one another.
- James 5:16—Pray for one another.

As They Arrive

Ask participants to letter their names on a name tag. Attach it shoulder level so it can easily be seen. Encourage them to select from the refreshment area and fellowship with each other for about eight to ten minutes. Suggest that they use statements that would model some of the "one anothers" from Scripture as they visit.

Share information

Ask participants to sit in groups of six to eight. Distribute handout with outline. Give three Scripture reference cards and Bibles to each group. Instruct them to read the Scriptures; identify the "one another" and then list on their handout at least three specific ways to live out that "one another" with students and ministry team members. Allow about fifteen minutes for this task.

Ask for volunteers to share from their lists for each of the nine Scriptures. With each list, discuss how that action would be of benefit to students or ministry team members. Encourage participants to add to their lists on the handout.

Plan to Use the Information

Distribute handout with heart shapes. Ask participants to write the name of a student or ministry teammate in each heart. Inside the heart, list actions that will be taken with that individual from the list of specific "one anothers."

Group Prayer and Planning Time

Focus on James 5:16—"Pray for one another." Take time to share specific prayer requests. Invest more time than usual in prayer.

Romans 12:10 may be used as a summary thought, "Be devoted to one another in brotherly love. Honor one another above yourselves." The very best learning for both students and volunteers will result when there is commitment to these words!

Use remaining time to work in ministry teams to plan for specific teaching sessions.

THE "ONE ANOTHERS" OF MINISTRY

John 13:34, 35—Love one another.

Romans 15:7—Accept one another.

Galatians 5:13—Serve one another.

Galatians 6:2—Bear one anothers' burdens.

Ephesians 4:32—Be kind and
forgive one another.

Ephesians 4:2—Be patient with
one another.

Colossians 3:16—Teach one another.

1 Thessalonians 5:11, 14—Encourage
one another.

James 5:16—Pray for one another.